CHIEF
★ OF ★
STAFF

Presidential chiefs of staff and moderator John Chancellor at the historic symposium "25 Years of the Presidency," held at the University of California, San Diego, in January 1986. Clockwise from top left: Richard Cheney, Harry McPherson, Donald Rumsfeld, Andrew Goodpaster, Jack Watson, Alexander Haig, John Chancellor, H. R. Haldeman, Theodore Sorensen.

Photo: Kira Corser.

CHIEF

★ OF ★

STAFF

TWENTY-FIVE YEARS OF
MANAGING THE PRESIDENCY

EDITED BY

Samuel Kernell and Samuel L. Popkin

FOREWORD BY

Richard E. Neustadt

University of California Press

BERKELEY   LOS ANGELES

LONDON

University of California Press
Berkeley and Los Angeles, California

University of California Press, Ltd.
London, England

Printed in the United States of America
1 2 3 4 5 6 7 8 9

Library of Congress Cataloging-in-Publication Data

Kernell, Samuel, 1945–
Chief of staff.

Includes index.
1. Presidents—United States—Staff.
I. Popkin, Samuel L.   II. Title.
JK518.K45   1986   353.03'2   86-16073
ISBN 0-520-05934-4 (alk. paper)

CONTENTS

FOREWORD

This book is unique. Not only does it offer anecdotes and observations widely interesting and nowhere else available about the conduct of the presidency of the United States, but also it conveys the thoroughgoing professionalism that has begun to characterize the people who immediately assist modern presidents. These senior aides may not go *in* as professionals but, as the men we encounter here betoken, they come out so. On the evidence of this book they come out—regardless of administration or political party—with a common ideal, a shared sense of duty, and agreed rules of the game, agreed at least with benefit of hindsight. These are buttressed by appreciation for the work and for the rules so strong as to spill over into fellow feeling for each other.

In that combination lies the professionalism. Here it is, on display. And while retrospective, those who share it are sufficiently dispersed geographically, sufficiently prominent in private life, and sufficiently well placed in politics, Democratic as well as Republican, so that their rules and their ideal may influence coming administrations early on.

This book is a step in that direction. The fast-paced

interchanges found here constitute a virtual "primer" for White House staff work. The primer does not focus on details of method or procedure but rather, more important, on do's and don'ts of personal approach toward the job, the president, one's colleagues, one's country, and one's own all-too-easily swelled head. Would-be White House aides, attentive to what lies between the lines of these conversations, will have taken a long step toward professionalism when they read this book. And if that reading takes place before they ever get near 1600 Pennsylvania Avenue, retrospect then becomes prospect, part of the book's promise.

But this book has far wider appeal than as a primer for prospective staffers. It offers an introduction to the attitudes, mind-sets, and work of some of the people who have played important parts, usually behind the scenes, in governing this country for the past quarter-century. It introduces also the positions from which they participated, the senior staff posts of significance in policy and politics, as well as in the president's own conduct of his daily chores, within the White House proper.

For half a century, since Franklin Roosevelt's time, there have been in every administration some three or four senior assistants, whose roles rivaled or outshone in policy significance (though not in protocol) those of even the department heads at State, Defense, Treasury, or Justice, the traditional inner cabinet posts. Under FDR in wartime, one thinks of Harry Hopkins, Samuel Rosenman, James Byrnes, and General "Pa" Watson. In Harry Truman's time, we had John Steelman, Matt Connolly, and Clark Clifford for the first term, Charles Murphy for the second. Under Dwight Eisenhower, Sherman Adams, Wilton Persons, Andrew Goodpaster, and James Hagerty spring to mind. For John Kennedy the "big three" were Theodore Sorensen, Kenneth O'Donnell, and McGeorge Bundy, with others a half-step behind. For LBJ, an early list would include Walter Jenkins, Bill Moyers, and again Bundy; later on, Joseph Califano and Harry McPherson, with one or two more. For Nixon the topmost seniors were H. R. Haldeman, John Ehrlichman, and Henry Kissinger; the first two were replaced toward the end by Kissinger's one-time deputy, Alexander Haig. In Ford's time the list begins with Kissinger and Donald Rumsfeld, succeeded by Brent Scowcroft and Richard Cheney, respectively. Carter's "big three" were Hamilton Jordan, Jody Powell, and increasingly Zbigniew Brzezinski, with Stuart Eizenstat a fourth and Jack Watson a fifth; toward the end Watson moved up. Ronald Reagan in his first term had two old hands, Edwin Meese and Michael Deaver, along with a new recruit, James Baker. A couple of others entered that circle as time went on: the big three became a big four and almost a big five. In Reagan's second term, uncharacteristically for him and for his predecessors, Reagan let Donald Regan, his chief of staff succeeding Baker, create a hierarchy so tight as to turn the big three or four into one, at least for the time being. This has not been seen before, save in the aftermath of Eisenhower's heart attack (and may indeed be transient).

Of those seniors among seniors, the topmost White House aides, this book records the lively views of eight, from the six administrations between Eisenhower and Carter. Reagan's senior people understandably declined to join in; FDR's and Truman's were no longer living or were otherwise unavailable. But a James Baker or a Clark Clifford would, I think, have reinforced the themes in the discussion and its overall impression of professionalism. They are among the ablest on the list, heroes indeed to the "profession." Still, without them both discussion and discussants remain representative. The profession has other heroes, several of whom were present, and the line of experience from Goodpaster to Watson is impressive enough in itself.

What these panelists have to say is fascinating for its own sake. The years from 1953 to 1981 are among the most dramatic in our modern history. Most of the events that made them so are at least mentioned here. The outlook from the West Wing of the White House in those years is what these men discuss, touching as they go on matters of the highest moment. For example, McPherson on LBJ, caught in the toils of Vietnam, "desperately trying to find the best way out of a tragic situation. Very much like Oedipus wishing he'd never met his father along the road."

Or Haldeman on his and Nixon's cover-up of Watergate:

> I think that we established . . . a superb staff-management system. . . . The thing I wish we had done was to have kept the system intact through the greatest crisis that did hit us. . . . The thing that went wrong is that the system was not followed. . . . Had we dealt with that matter [Watergate] in the way we set up from the outset . . . within a few weeks we would have resolved that matter satisfactorily overall, probably unfortunately for some people but that was necessary and should have been done. It wasn't done and that led to the ultimate crisis.

By implication, a former attorney general and at least two White House aides should have been found out and handed to the Justice Department in July or August 1972. In short, *mea culpa*—and a hard issue of timing.

Every such comment in these transcripts is packed with implications, and there are such comments on almost every page. Talking to one another these men use shorthand. Readers less acquainted with events will miss much of the relevance and richness of the interchange unless they pause to put each comment into context. If they do, the insights gained should more than repay the effort. Besides, the book moves so fast that reading it is always fun—and will, I don't doubt, generate its own enthusiasm for going farther.

Also, readers will notice how the thinking of the commentators has been shaped by experience, and not only their experience as seniors at the White House. Here is General Haig, Nixon's last chief of staff (and Reagan's first secretary of state) recalling Johnson's situation at the time of the Tonkin Gulf incident: "[He] was engaged much too early, when we just had very fuzzy intelligence reports." At the time Haig was a staff assistant to the secretary of defense in a Democratic administration, five years before he first went to Nixon's White House.

The only one of the discussants here whose White House work was not informed by prior government experience is Haldeman; for that he suffered personally, and his president as well, to say nothing of the country. In this book no one dwells upon the prices paid for covering up Watergate, or on adverse results from the mistakes of other sorts in other administrations. But plenty of them are alluded to, some for the first time publicly. As their facial expressions and occasional exclamations revealed, all the discussants knew and could judge costs—indeed, no doubt, had long since done so—on one another's watch. Their demeanor toward each other, courtesy not contest, was the order of the day: part of their professionalism in bipartisan proceedings. But as mistakes succeed each other in convivial reminiscence, readers should not imagine that these people were unaware of implications, insensitive to consequences. When Watson, for example, says, "All our problems in the transition of 1976 were self-imposed. . . . problems of integrating campaign staff with transition planners . . . to some extent, with Hamilton Jordan and myself," I do not doubt that everybody present understood his references, filled in the blanks, and had strong views about the rights and wrongs of it all.

The pace and content of the discussions owe much to the moderator of the conference's first session: John Chancellor. His thoughtfulness, backed by what must have been extensive homework, is embodied in his opening question, which got things off to a rousing start: "How do you talk a president out of a damn fool idea?" The influence of that strong start, the interest he established, carried through the second and third sessions as well. As an academic questioner (with *junior* staff experience from Truman's time) who had been asked to help begin the third session, I know how much Chancellor's contribution mattered even then, when he himself was silent. The organizers of this conference, ingenious throughout, were especially ingenious when they chose him.

Fifty years ago, before World War II, the White House was primarily a residence, as it had been since Thomas Jefferson moved in. The West Wing, an extension built in Theodore Roosevelt's time, contained an oval office for the president and also housed three or four senior aides, along with perhaps half a dozen junior aides who had some share (beyond the strictly clerical) in presidential business. Today the senior staff has swelled to ten or twelve, including *senior* seniors, the "big three" (or one), and relatively junior staff now number almost forty. Adjacent to the White House is another presidential agency, the Office of Management and Budget, which in 1936 had fewer than thirty staffers above clerical rank and since World War II has rarely had fewer than four hundred. Still other agencies, collectively employing at least half as many, are arrayed around those two. This has been the situation for a generation. Kennedy was the last president to have a staff on the scale of Truman's—and Truman's had been twice the size of Roosevelt's before the war.

The growth has been partly a matter of functions transferred, during the last half of this century, from their traditional places in executive departments to the White House itself. Presidential staff work used to be done mainly by the staffs of cabinet officers, if done at all. Now it has been centralized. Eisenhower outfitted the White House with its own congressional relations staff. He also launched, and Nixon vastly expanded, the modern national security staff. Johnson built, and Nixon again expanded, a domestic policy staff. Reagan has completed what Nixon contemplated: White House staff control of all appointive jobs, which once were mostly left to cabinet members.

Technology has done the rest. The shift from print to electronic media as primary news sources brought a fourfold increase in the staffs for press and communications. The shift from trains to planes and helicopters, raising presidential mobility, had a comparable effect on aides for scheduling and travel, especially as security problems also rose. And so forth.

The president now has his own department. At its apex is the White House office. Counting only aides above the technical and clerical, that staff is now three times the size of Truman's.

It is no wonder that another Eisenhower innovation —temporarily suspended under Kennedy and Johnson— has remained in effect since Nixon restored it (except for Carter's first two years): a chief of staff, sometimes without that title, as administrative coordinator of internal personnel decisions, space and work assignments, paper flows, external contacts, and dealings with the president. The chief of staff has always been one of the topmost aides, a senior among seniors, but his responsibilities in policy and politics have varied more from one administration to another (or from year to year) than have those relatively obvious administrative duties. The latter are anchored in staff size; the former wax or wane with personalities and with the president's own interests or energies from time to time.

Even so, the White House chief of staff becomes an officer of high importance to our constitutional system. He (or someday she) is nowhere mentioned in the Constitution, where the president stands alone. The duties of the chief of staff derive from nothing more than personal delegation. Constitutionally he is and has to be the president's mere dogsbody, to borrow a British term. Practically, however, he cannot help being more than that. For while he holds his boss's confidence he will be, in effect, a presidential deputy, sometimes even a substitute.

In Washington this now seems understood, less so outside. Members of Congress, executive officials, and reporters seemingly accept it even in the somewhat special case of Reagan's Regan. But among citizens at large there seems to be less understanding, also in some quarters less acceptance. And in political circles beyond Washington, the case may be the same. As recently as 1977, a president not previously experienced "inside the Beltway" came there personally determined to abolish the job. So Carter initially did. Had a book of just this sort then been available it might have given him pause. It might also have kept the question, whether to have a chief of staff, out of partisan politics. Instead of a stick with which to beat Ford and Nixon, the job might have been taken for what it has become, a virtual necessity, at least in its administrative dimension.

From now on it is reasonable to hope that the next victorious candidate arriving at the White House without Washington experience will know enough to read this book—or that reporters and constituents who have read it themselves will force it on him. And that goes double for the campaign aides he brings in with him. They, above all, need the stories, the vicarious experience, this book conveys. More even than that, they need the ideal and the rules.

Richard E. Neustadt
Harvard University
Cambridge, Massachusetts
May 1986

PREFACE

Much has been written and yet relatively little is known about the inner workings of the White House office. To allow the public a glimpse into this most powerful administrative preserve, the University of California at San Diego, along with members of the nonacademic community, brought together for the first time eight former chiefs of staff, representing the six administrations from President Eisenhower to President Carter.

In a televised symposium and subsequent roundtable discussions with journalists and scholars, these once-powerful insiders illuminate for us the human side of the White House office—the importance of one man's decisions and the pressures faced by his senior aides. In the course of these two days of discussions, we also witness a singular kinship develop among these former chiefs of staff, a professional bond that transcends the politics and the individual styles of the presidents they served.

The symposium would have been neither as electric nor as effective without the assistance of John Chancellor, who moderated the proceedings, and KPBS, the public television station at San Diego State University. The KPBS videotape of the first session, which was broadcast nationally by the Public Broadcasting Service, and an instructor's guide are available to teachers and libraries through the Extension Services of the University of California, San Diego.

It was my exceptional pleasure to be involved in formulating the concept for the symposium and in cajoling the participants to attend. I think you will find that they enjoyed it as much as we did.

Gerald L. Warren
Editor, *San Diego Union*

ACKNOWLEDGMENTS

Gerald Warren, editor of the *San Diego Union* and former deputy press secretary to Presidents Nixon and Ford, conceived the idea for this symposium and introduced many of the participants to our university. Had he not lent his prestige to this endeavor, the symposium would have never been attempted. He also helped us balance the demands of a public forum against the longer-term goals of stimulating new academic research about the White House.

Mary Walshok, associate vice-chancellor for extended studies and public service, University of California, San Diego, served as our impressario, coordinating the many parts of our symposium and putting all the ideas into action.

John Chancellor, NBC news correspondent, provided us with a master class in the art of interviewing. His knowledge of the modern presidency and his instinctive sense of the underlying currents were essential to the symposium's success in distilling so much of the last twenty-five years into two days of discussions. Each time we reread the transcript, we gain new appreciation for his artistry.

Dianne Kernell provided the background notes for these discussions and developed an instructor's guide to accompany the videotape of the proceedings. Jacqueline Scoones, of the UC San Diego Development Office, managed the logistics. Viviane Pratt, chair of the KPBS-TV Community Advisory Committee, inspired us to make arrangements to have the first session of the symposium videotaped for public television. The program was coproduced by Peter Kaye, associate editor of the *San Diego Union*, and Sarah Luft of KPBS-TV; George Kelly and Larry Davis assisted with research.

We would also like to acknowledge the financial support of the following corporations and individuals: UCSD Chancellor's Associates; UCSD Extension; UCSD Extension ARCO Foundation Fund; KPBS Television; KPBS Radio; the Price Family Foundation; Dr. Gene W. Ray; Viviane Pratt; Titan Corporation, Dr. Gene W. Ray, president and chief executive officer; Management Analysis Corporation, Robert Stinson, president; Photon Research Associates, Inc., James A. Meyer, president; Verac Incorporated, Dr. Jeff Nash, chairman of the board; Systems Exploration Incorporated, Mike Jenkins, president; QUALCOMM Incorporated, Irwin Jacobs, president; and Mrs. Helen K. Copley.

Samuel Kernell
Samuel L. Popkin

THE ART OF
MANAGING THE WHITE HOUSE

The symposium held at the University of California, San Diego as part of its twenty-fifth anniversary celebration brought together for the first time eight former White House chiefs of staff, members of the innermost circle of presidential advisors. These two days of discussion are filled with anecdotes that allow us to savor and appreciate the nuances of a delicate and difficult job. The participants largely ignore the political differences between their administrations or parties and focus instead on their ideas and ideals about the art and craft of operating as senior managers in the White House. These conversations thus represent the distilled wisdom of our last six presidential administrations and set forth the professional standards these men learned in the political trenches.

The transcripts presented here have been lightly edited: several brief and unproductive forays into topics beyond the scope of the conference (for example, a discussion of the two-term limit on the presidency) and various nonsubstantive procedural details and introductions have been deleted. We have also made the small syntactical emendations necessary to transform an oral discourse into a written document, and two patches of conversation were relocated in order to bring together complementary discussions. A handful of editorial interpolations, restricted to the identification of persons or organizations, are enclosed in brackets.

The Executive Office of the President includes the White House staff, the Office of Management and Budget (OMB), the Council of Economic Advisors, the National Security Council (NSC), domestic policy staff, and many smaller units. The White House staff proper includes counselors, assistants, a press office, a personnel office, and a congressional liaison office. In the past quarter of a century the White House staff has ranged from 400 to 650 persons, the OMB staff from 450 to 700 persons, and the NSC staff from 55 to 85 persons.

The chief of staff—or the president's inner circle in the absence of an officially designated chief—is responsible for coordinating and directing the flow of papers and visitors to the president's office. In recent decades the expanding role of the chief of staff has been part of one of the most significant developments in modern American government: the centralization of power and influence in the White House staff and the Office of Management and Budget.

The increase in the size of the White House staff does not alone explain the increase in the influence and prominence of its senior members. Rather, as the panel's discussions detail, both the size and the prominence of the White House staff have grown in response to dramatic changes in the relation of the president to the federal government, to Congress, and to the American people. More specifically, the chiefs cite the development of communications technology, the growth of government and congressional staffs, and the demands of the presidential primary system.

Live global satellite transmissions, for example, and the dominance of television as our national news medium place ever-greater demands on the president. When a crisis occurs anywhere in the world, the White House can instantaneously communicate with persons who are on the spot and can immediately join in the deliberations, whether the issue is a change of government in Haiti or the Philippines, civil unrest in Johannesburg, or a military incident in Korea or Kampuchea. Instantaneous communications technology thus creates new demands for instant expertise in the White House. The president must have immediate access to information about every part of the globe, and he must have advisors in the White House who can provide immediate interpretations from a presidential point of view.

These instantaneous relays to the president from on-the-spot observers and commanders disrupt the traditional channels of information and the chain of command in the decision process. During crises presidents receive the very latest information directly from the field, before anyone else in the government. This inevitably leads, as Alexander Haig points out, to decision making that excludes the echelons of experienced observers of a problem. The specialists who do not yet have access to the last minute of information cannot address the president's concerns. President Ford, as Richard Cheney and Donald Rumsfeld recount, received information about the *Mayaguez* from a pilot flying over Kampuchean waters before reports had reached either the naval commanders in the area or most of the planners in the Pentagon.

While telecommunications allow instant international contact, television daily focuses the nation's attention on one or two issues or events. All White House activity comes to a standstill during the evening network news, as everyone watches to see which problems or incidents are treated as lead stories and which are the subject of special feature pieces. The panelists' anecdotes and observations confirm that the day in 1963 when network news was extended to thirty minutes will be seen as a critical day in the history of the modern presidency.

Returning to the issue of the size of the White House staff, we need only note that the president and his staff must deal with the staffs of every member of the House and Senate and their legislative committees, and that congressional staffs have tripled in size in the last twenty-five years. For a president to make substantial cuts in his staff would require simultaneous reductions in force on the other side of the Hill, as well. A president may occasionally make small cuts in the White House, but permanent reductions will entail negotiations with Congress that might approach the complexity of discussions on arms limitations with Russia.

Finally, the expansion of the presidential primary system and a concurrent weakening and splintering of national party organizations have pressed the White House to take a larger role in managing the politics of the president's party. Each year a growing number of well-financed lobbies and grass-roots groups must be heard and reckoned with if the president and his party's local and statewide candidates are to be reelected. As Richard Cheney notes, nothing better helps the mind to focus on priorities than "a thirteen-hundred-vote victory in the New Hampshire primary."

Whether it is the Bay of Pigs, a hostage crisis, or the New Hampshire primary, a chief of staff organizes the flow of information to and from the Oval Office. Why, then, do these men who manage the staff of the most powerful person in the world deny that they have power? How are we to interpret these denials from men who, as David Broder notes, in other times and places have engaged in political plots against a recalcitrant Congress or an uncooperative cabinet, even in plots against the president himself in order to prevail in getting him to do or not do something they thought he should or should not be doing?

The chiefs speak of themselves as personally powerless, as merely carrying out the president's orders because they value both loyalty to their bosses and personal anonymity. Indeed, this loyalty to the man from whom their power derives is so taken for granted that it is seldom mentioned. When President Eisenhower was speechless and bedridden after his heart attack, and could only nod his head yes or no to memos presented to him by his aides, General Goodpaster insists that he and the other members of the inner circle were only doing what the president wanted.

When in office a chief's denial of having personal power is essential to maximizing his power and his boss's success. A White House staffer who becomes too prominent or appears too powerful detracts from the record of his boss. As Richard Cheney notes, Henry Kissinger was removed as head of President Ford's National Security Council because he had made himself too visible and was getting too much credit—and the president not enough—for international affairs, not because there was dissatisfaction with his policies.

Although a chief's power is derived from his boss's power, it is, of course, patently false that these men, despite their loyalty, exercised no independent power. Even if they never sought to directly influence their bosses by giving advice, their management of the traffic in and out of the Oval Office enabled them to exert a decisive influence on decisions. Some of the most important lessons in the art of presidential management contained in these transcripts deal with the critical role of "counterbalancing" in presidential decision making. The chiefs see it as a chief's responsibility to ensure that the president does not act until he has talked with all his advisors. Though this procedure is called "staffing out a decision," with the chief of staff acting as an "honest broker," a chief's counterbalancing is an exercise of power. The chiefs simply label their influence in such matters as the benign "providing of inputs," ensuring that the president is fully briefed by an array of advisors before he acts. Counterbalancing requires that the chief be seen as an honest broker, but whenever a chief introduces another advisor, he may be diminishing the power of the advisors whom the president has already consulted.

As Donald Rumsfeld notes, because President Nixon was particularly fond of Treasury Secretary John Connally and enjoyed talking with him, Bob Haldeman had to figure out ways to make sure that the president heard the views of other senior administration advisors on economics—Paul McCracken, Herb Stein, George Shultz, and Arthur Burns—before he made decisions about economic policy. Presumably, to John Connally and members of his staff, Haldeman looked like a man with power, not just a counterbalancer. Conversely, President Ford did not personally enjoy Secretary of Defense James Schlesinger's company, although he respected him, and the chief of staff therefore had to make sure that Schlesinger's views were heard alongside those of Secretary of State Kissinger. Presumably, to Kissinger this looked like an arrogant seizure of power by a White House minion; but Kissinger knew that he needed the chief's goodwill if his memos were to be delivered to the president in a timely fashion.

A chief of staff's power thus derives from his ability to schedule the president's time, allocate access to him, and shape his agenda. There is always more than one critical memo waiting for the president, always more than one important phone call to return, and always more than one dispute to settle. As Theodore Sorensen observes, what really matters is not who has a White House parking permit or who uses the White House tennis courts, but who is allowed to invoke the president's name or use his telephone or stationery.

Cabinet members can be so starved for the president's time, as Gerald Warren notes, that one will pull out his agenda when he meets the president in a receiving line after church. The art of chiefsmanship, above all, depends on judgments about timing, knowing when to bring the White House or the president into an issue and knowing when to bring other members of the government to the president.

Implicit in every anecdote in these transcripts is an awareness of the multiple constituencies and goals that vie for a president's limited time and energy. Most executive decisions involve more than one cabinet member, provoke some congressional opposition from members of the president's own party, evoke outcries from friendly and unfriendly constituencies, and have important international repercussions. Each interested cabinet member, politician, leader, and ambassador hopes to derive personal benefits and benefits to the cause by making a case directly to the president. At the same time, the president is working on other equally important issues as well as fulfilling ceremonial exigencies, entertaining visiting dignitaries, granting interviews, and planning for press conferences.

As the pointman in rationing and allocating the president's time, the chief of staff may appear to be deciding the outcome by the way he sets the agenda. But when the chief does not oversee access to the president, the balance among constituencies may be upset. As Donald Rumsfeld tells us, when Gerald Ford and Secretary of Labor John Dunlop discussed changes in the laws governing the picketing of construction sites, neither the chief of staff nor any other White House staffer was present. Dunlop then independently worked out an understanding on the legislation with organized labor, but Ford could not finally support the agreement once his staff advised him that he had underestimated the effect of the legislation on other constituencies. As this example shows, serving the president does not mean simply enforcing loyalty or forcing cabinet members to place the president's interests ahead of their own, although this too occurs. No one cabinet member, however loyal, can adequately assess the views of all the constituencies that the president must deal with. The comprehensive vista that the president must have can come only from the White House staff.

Sometimes, too, the pointman becomes the fall guy. Donald Rumsfeld describes how he took a rap to preserve harmony between President Ford and a cabinet member who was upset at having been left off the guest list for a state dinner. If the cabinet member were not at the dinner, it would appear that he had been downgraded and it would be harder for him to convince recalcitrants in Congress and the bureaucracy to back his policies. All the cabinet member's efforts could unravel just because he was not seen at a dinner. Rumsfeld relayed news of the oversight to the president, but Ford let the matter drop until the affronted cabinet member mentioned it to him directly. The President feigned surprise and immediately added him to the list, leaving the cabinet member to assume that Rumsfeld had simply decided not to relay the message and to cut him out of the negotiations by that signal. In just this way, chiefs may often appear to be exercising independent judgment in cases in which what they are really doing is covering someone else's oversights or errors in judgment.

Indeed, social occasions pose particular problems for the president, as each possible repercussion needs to be staffed out, as though a dinner or a party were tantamount to a summit conference or a round of treaty negotiations. When Speaker of the House Tip O'Neill invited his old friend Gerry Ford to a birthday party, the president promptly accepted, unaware that the man giving the party was under investigation for influence peddling. The chief of staff had to convince him to stay away from his friend's party.

In Washington circles, careers can be made merely by dining with or hosting the president, and careers can be broken by a random off-the-cuff remark.

Are chiefs of staff really necessary? The Watergate cover-up revealed the dangers of a closed White House. As a reaction against these dangers, Presidents Ford and Carter each were determined to act as the chief of staff and to have a number of senior advisors report directly to the president. The "spokes-of-the-wheel" system inevitably broke down, however, because it did not allow adequate counterbalancing or staffing out of problems, it brought problems to the president's desk too quickly, and it overextended the president's energies.

Chiefs are necessary, it seems, because a president's time must be rationed, decisions must be paced, and access by the staff and cabinet need to be refereed. Despite the growth of government and presidential powers and responsibilities since 1776, despite the rise of the welfare state, the invention of telecommunications, and the development of presidential primaries, the length of a president's day has remained twenty-four hours. In addition, chiefs can sometimes learn what presidents cannot. As John Kennedy's staff found out during the Cuban Missile Crisis, only when the president is absent from a meeting will assistants challenge their bosses; in front of the president, assistants will not contradict or question their immediate superiors.

Just as a state dinner illustrates how even the smallest access to the president can be critical to a cabinet member, the politics of writing a speech illustrates the problems of daily management that the chiefs confront. Speechwriters are well aware that their drafts will be given to administration officials for a review of the text's policy implications. When a cabinet member changes a phrase to alter the content—whether to help the president or to further some personal cause—the speechwriter may resent the lexical mutilation thereby inflicted. To protect their artistry and handicraft from "mere" substantive concerns, speechwriters sometimes stall on turning in their drafts. To the chief of staff is left the task of appeasing the speechwriters while making sure that policy, not rhetoric, determines what the president says.

The craft of the chiefs and the value of experience is most apparent when they discuss timing, when to bring the president into an issue. Although a Monday-morning quarterback might most readily cite cases in which a president's involvement came too late, the chiefs are aware of the dangers of both premature and belated involvement. Dwight Eisenhower at first acted unconcerned when the USSR beat America into space with a satellite; a groundswell of near-panic, abetted by the Democrats, forced him to change his approach. Had Jimmy Carter become publicly involved too early at Three Mile Island, however, he might have created a panic. Waking a president in the middle of the night can escalate an incident into a crisis, but to let him sleep through is to run the risk that he will be perceived as remote from breaking events.

Internal affairs must also be paced. To bring in a cabinet member for discussions with the president before the other concerned interests are ready to present their alternatives wastes the president's time; the cabinet member will only have to return, and the first visit could have been devoted to another issue or constituency. Once the press knows that an issue is on the president's desk, the pressure for statements and action begins. Again, bringing an issue into the Oval Office prematurely can interfere with serious deliberation and effective staffing.

The chiefs believe that their own effectiveness depends on their credibility with cabinet secretaries, legislators, and various constituents. All these parties must believe that the chief of staff is a fair, objective, nonpartisan manager with only the president's interests in mind. The chiefs also care about carefully defining the inner circle, about who briefs the president or who orders the memos in his in-basket. Such concerns arise not to gratify their own hunger for status but to maintain solidarity in the face of constant onslaughts and temptations for partisanship. The hardest situations for a chief of staff to handle are conflicts between a White House staffer and a member of the administration who is outside the White House, such as the struggle between NSC head Zbigniew Brzezinski and Secretary of State Cyrus Vance in the Carter administration.

In the following pages readers will discover the artistry of eight men who have at one time managed the largest corporation in the world. Readers too, will hear Jack Watson's response when pressed for an analogy: Is the White House chief of staff most like a quarterback, a goalie, or a utility infielder? "More like being a javelin catcher," he assures us.

Samuel L. Popkin
University of California, San Diego
La Jolla, California
May 1986

LIST OF PARTICIPANTS

General Andrew J. Goodpaster. After serving for five years as President Dwight Eisenhower's White House staff secretary, General Goodpaster assumed many of the duties of the chief of staff in 1958 and stayed on for the first two months of President Kennedy's term. During Eisenhower's term, General Goodpaster supervised the National Security Council staff, briefed the president on intelligence matters, and was White House liaison for defense and national security. A career army officer, Goodpaster served as supreme allied commander in Europe from 1969 to 1974. In 1977 he was recalled from retirement and appointed superintendent of the U.S. Military Academy at West Point.

Theodore C. Sorensen. Sorensen served Senator John F. Kennedy as a special assistant from 1953 to 1961 and was appointed White House counsel when Kennedy became president. He was the president's principal advisor on domestic issues and was involved in the handling of the Cuban Missile Crisis as well. He remained in the White House during the early months of the Johnson administration and then joined a law firm in New York, where he continues to practice. He has written three books about the Kennedy era and one about Watergate.

Harry C. McPherson. McPherson was appointed special assistant and counsel to President Lyndon Johnson in 1965 and special counsel to the president in 1966. He advised the president on legislation and was White House liaison with the Congress and the Justice Department on civil rights and urban affairs. His prior government service included posts as counsel to the Democratic policy committee in the Senate, deputy under secretary of the army, and assistant secretary of state. He is now an attorney in Washington, D.C. and vice-chairman and general counsel to the John F. Kennedy Center for the Performing Arts.

H. R. Haldeman. After directing Richard M. Nixon's campaign for the presidency in 1968, Haldeman served President Nixon as chief of staff from 1969 to 1973; he subsequently served a prison term for his part in the Watergate cover-up. Earlier Haldeman had played key roles in Nixon's campaigns for the vice-presidency in 1956, the presidency in 1960, and the California governorship in 1962. He is now president of a Los Angeles hotel corporation.

General Alexander M. Haig. General Haig was deputy to National Security Advisor Henry Kissinger during the early days of President Nixon's administration. He became President Nixon's chief of staff in 1973, after the resignation of H. R. Haldeman, and he remained in that post during the first weeks of President Gerald Ford's term. In 1974 General Haig succeeded General Goodpaster as supreme commander of NATO, a post he held until 1979, when he resigned to enter private industry. General Haig returned to government service as secretary of state for the first eighteen months of President Ronald Reagan's first term.

Donald Rumsfeld. Rumsfeld succeeded General Haig as staff coordinator during President Ford's administration. His responsibilities included supervising personnel appointments, overseeing the policy-making process, and preparing the president for press conferences. Fifteen months later, in November 1975, he was named to the cabinet as secretary of defense. Before joining the Ford White House, he had been sent by Illinois voters to three terms in the House of Representatives, been director of the Office of Economic Opportunity and White House counselor during the Nixon administration, and served as ambassador to NATO. He is now the chief executive officer of a pharmaceuticals corporation in Chicago.

Richard B. Cheney. Cheney was named as President Ford's staff coordinator in September 1975 and served until the end of Ford's term. Before that, he had been a congressional aide, deputy director at the Office of Economic Opportunity, assistant director of the Cost of Living Council, and deputy staff coordinator for the White House. He is now in his fourth term as Wyoming's sole member of the House of Representatives, where he chairs the Republican policy committee.

Jack H. Watson, Jr.   Watson became President Jimmy Carter's chief of staff in 1980 when Hamilton Jordan resigned to manage the president's reelection committee. From 1972 to 1977 Watson was chairman of the board of the Georgia Department of Human Resources. He first joined the White House staff as head of Carter's transition team in 1976, then served as coordinator of intergovernmental affairs, secretary to the cabinet, and coordinator of urban policy. Since leaving Washington, D.C. he has been a partner in an Atlanta law firm and has published several articles on social and mental health issues.

★ 1 ★

Up on the Bridge
and Down in the Engine Room

The two-day conference opened with a panel discussion among eight former White House chiefs of staff. The proceedings were moderated by John Chancellor, long-time political correspondent and commentator, former anchorman of the "NBC Nightly News," and himself a student of the presidency. Before the session, Mr. Chancellor had informed the participants of the nature of his first question, but they had no prior knowledge of the other questions he had prepared.

This panel discussion was held on the morning of January 17, 1986, at the Mandell Weiss Center for the Performing Arts at the University of California, San Diego. In the audience were members of the university community, invited scholars, members of the international press corps, and a camera crew from the Public Broadcasting System (PBS). Two hour-long selections from those videotapes were first shown on PBS stations across the country in June 1986.

John Chancellor: Today we have assembled eight men who have never before gathered together. They are here to discuss an experience which for them, and for the rest of us, was very important. Each of them played critically important roles in the running of the White House. They had different titles, but for simplicity's sake, we will call them and we will deal with them as eight former chiefs of staff. Six presidents, from Eisenhower to Carter, depended on their advice.

We have asked them here to talk about the presidency, about changes in the White House over a quarter of a century, about their own memorable moments, and about the future of this awesome office.

"Damn fool" ideas and "oh, by the way" decisions

Chancellor: Presidents are human. Presidents make mistakes. Sometimes presidents want to do damn fool things they have to be talked out of, and so my question to all of you to begin this panel today is: How do you talk a president out of a damn fool idea?

Harry McPherson: Well, very gingerly—(*laughter*)—if your president is Lyndon Johnson.

One morning in 1968, I was at home, and President Johnson called me, outraged because I had sent in a list of cities where I thought we might meet with the North Vietnamese. He didn't want to meet at any of those cities, and he said he was about to announce that he would not meet at any of those cities; if they wanted to meet with him, they could meet—I don't know—San Diego or someplace like that. (*Laughter*)

And I was very tired. I had been up late the night before and had been working with Clark Clifford on this list.[1] Well, I let go and yelled at the president on the phone as loud as I could and for a long time. I called him a lot of rough names. My wife ran down the stairs in dismay because she thought I was talking to the plumber. That's true, and she thought I was going to drive the guy away. (*Laughter*)

When I hung up, I called Clark Clifford to warn him that the president had just called me and had raised hell about this, and he said to his long-time secretary, Miss Wiler—he asked me what time I'd finished talking, and I said, "Exactly 8:30, he called"—and he said, "Miss Wiler, what time did I finish with the President?" Back came the word, "8:29."

So you do it very carefully. You do it with a conviction that what you are doing is in the national interest and very much in the president's political interest.

Donald Rumsfeld: I think it depends on the president, how you argue or discuss an issue like that.

I can recall President Ford meeting privately with

---

1. Clark Clifford assumed the post of secretary of defense in March 1968, following Robert McNamara's resignation in February. The formal peace talks began in Paris on May 10, 1968, and continued for almost five years, until a ceasefire was agreed to on January 27, 1973.

one of his senior officials in the administration and, in effect, coming away with an agreement that he would put forward to the Congress a proposal which had not been staffed out at all and which, in my view, was not very wise—and that is a massive understatement. The way it was finally accomplished was simply by staffing it out. In other words, taking this idea and putting it into the staff system—the people that he had hired and brought aboard, who in some cases had statutory authority over that area of government—and letting them then provide their advice and allowing some time so that he could have the benefit of their views.

Chancellor: Isn't that called stalling? (*Laughter*)

Rumsfeld: No. I would call it professional staff work. But sometimes it takes very, very long. (*Laughter*)

Richard Cheney: President Ford, of course, because of his personality and his service in Congress, welcomed the debate and the dialogue. You were free at any time to go into the Oval Office and argue with him about something, and he would agree or disagree, and then you could come back two hours later and do it again. He never denied you access because you argued with him.

The biggest problem was the decision that didn't receive attention. It wasn't so much a matter of his making a damn fool decision, as you said, John, as it was his making some kind of offhand decision that hadn't been carefully thought about, and then people took it and ran with it. It's what I called an "Oh, by the way" decision.

It was the kind of thing that would happen when

somebody was cleared to go into the Oval Office, a cabinet member, to talk about a subject; the president was prepared. They had their discussion, and as the cabinet member was leaving, he'd turn around and he'd say, "Oh, by the way, Mr. President," and then bring up a totally unrelated subject, get a decision on it, and run with it. That's when you really got into big trouble.

Chancellor: Mr. Haldeman, it has been written that when President Nixon would give you certain kinds of instructions, you'd say "Yes, sir," and then go off and start a process which didn't always result in that action being taken. Can you tell us about that?

H. R. Haldeman: I don't think I'm unique among this group. (*Laughter*) I suspect that we all shared that kind of activity fairly frequently. But that, I think, is essential; however, it depends on the relationship between the staff person who's making that kind of move and the president himself, because the president has got to feel that there are some people with whom he can explore rather than command, and that in exploring, he's going to raise some things that don't, to him, at the moment he's raising them, seem like damn fool things but could very well turn out to be that or seem so after second thought.

It's the obligation of the staff and the function of the staff to pose the alternatives. Carrying that a step further, I think, it's the obligation of the senior staff person dealing with any such kind of a situation not to carry out the order until it has been at least reviewed once and then reordered by the president on the basis of making the right decision for the right reasons instead of for the wrong reasons.

The staff function, as we saw it, was to get the proper information to the president, and then the president made the decision. Once the president has made the decision on the proper basis, then it does have to be carried out.

Chancellor: Wasn't there one time, though, when he said to you, "Bob, you never did that, did you?" and you said, "No, sir, I didn't"?

Haldeman: Yes, there was. And it's interesting because it's been repeated not too far back in time now.

I was ordered by the president unequivocally and immediately to commence lie detector tests of every employee of the State Department because there had been a series of leaks which were seriously damaging our negotiations in Vietnam.[2] It was a very serious

---

2. Concerned with press leaks, particularly in the realm of foreign policy, Nixon authorized the FBI to tap the private telephones of Henry Kissinger's National Security Council staff in 1969. In 1970 Nixon approved a proposal to establish an interagency intelligence group to stop security leaks; when FBI Director J. Edgar Hoover strongly objected, the plan was dropped. In June 1971 the White House established a covert investigative unit, "the plumbers." A leak to the *New York Times* about the secret bombing of Cambodia prompted the White House to order additional wiretaps, but they failed to link anyone with the leaks. See Richard Nixon, *The Memoirs of Richard Nixon* (New York: Grosset & Dunlap, 1978), pp. 386–88; Henry Kissinger, *White House Years* (Boston: Little, Brown, 1979), pp. 250–53 and *Years of Upheaval* (Boston: Little, Brown, 1982), pp. 421–22.

The issue of lie detector tests arose again in December 1985, when President Reagan issued two directives ordering polygraph examinations for all government employees with high security clearance or access to sensitive information. Secretary of State George Shultz, among others, threatened to resign if the directives were implemented, and the orders were soon modified.

problem. The order to solve the problem was that every member of the State Department staff *worldwide* was to be submitted *immediately* to lie detector tests. That was an easy order not to carry out because it was physically impossible to do. It couldn't have been done anyway. But we didn't do it, and the president said the next day, "Have you gotten a lie detector program started?" And I said no, and he said, "Aren't you going to?" And I said, "I don't intend to," and he again ordered that it be done.

I again didn't do it on the first round that time, then went back to him later that day, and after that time—Al is smirking over here, because Haig remembers this perhaps more vividly than I do—I went back and said, "Mr. President, this really is a mistake. There are other ways of dealing with this problem at this point, and we will be back to you with a plan for doing that." We came back in a few days with a plan, and he said at that point, "I didn't think you would do it." (*Laughter*) But it was fairly clear at the time that I was supposed to.

Chancellor: General Goodpaster, you worked for one of the great historical figures of American life, way up there on Mount Rushmore, President Eisenhower. Did you ever have a comparable experience with him?

General Andrew Goodpaster: Somewhat comparable, I think. He came over one morning rather exasperated and said, "I've said that I want to start reducing our forces in Europe. You know that's our policy, and I want action to be initiated on that." I said, "Well, Mr. President, it isn't quite our policy."

"What do you mean?"

I said, "Well, that's the goal that's stated—to work down to the long-term strength—but it's conditioned on the ability of the Europeans to fill the gap that's there, the gap we created."

"No," he said, "that's not right. Our policy is to make that reduction and I want to get that started."

I said, "Well, Mr. President, that really isn't the policy. It's conditioned in this way." (*Laughter*) He glared at me and he said, "I've got Foster Dulles coming over here today, and I'm going to have him straighten you out on this."[3]

Well, I didn't say a word to Secretary Dulles when he came over. We went in together, and the president looked up and he said, "Foster, I want you to straighten Andy out on this once and for all. It *is* our policy to reduce those forces in Europe." And Foster Dulles, bless him, said, "Well, Mr. President, it isn't quite that clear. We always have put that condition on it, that the Europeans have to be able to fill that gap." The president looked up at Foster Dulles and he said, "Foster, I've lost my last friend." (*Laughter*)

But I think we both knew that that was our duty, and the president knew it perfectly well. He just was sounding off, and that was part of our role in life, to

---

3. A fiscal conservative, Eisenhower was acutely aware of the financial burden of maintaining U.S. troops in Europe. Secretary of State John Foster Dulles and many others in the security community insisted, however, that any reduction of U.S. troop strength in NATO had to be matched by increases in European troops.

let him relieve some of the pressure, but make sure that he didn't make that kind of a mistake.

Chancellor: Jack Watson, Jimmy Carter had a reputation as a president who knew practically everything, did a lot of homework, read all the papers. But coming out of all that work he did, all that midnight oil, did he ever come in the office and say, "Hey, we're going to send General Custer to the Little Big Horn tomorrow morning"?

Jack Watson: No, but he said he felt lust in his heart. (*Laughter*)

I remember very well—Dick Cheney, who is sitting over there smirking right now, also remembers—in the campaign of 1976. It was coming down to the wire, Carter was ahead in the polls, and then he had the infamous *Playboy* magazine interview in which he made that comment, and we plummeted in the polls and then, interestingly enough, recovered.[4]

I think I very much agree with something that Dick Cheney and that Don Rumsfeld said a moment ago. The most important thing that the chief of staff can do in terms of protecting against the "damn fool de-

---

4. One account offers the following assessment: "As Carter had convinced the electorate of his superior morality, the shock to some of the people was all the greater when the notorious interview with him appeared in the November 1976 issue of *Playboy*, in which he confessed that he had lusted in his heart after women and employed such otherwise common words as 'screw' and 'shack up.'" John Tebbel and Sarah Miles Watts, *The Press and the Presidency* (New York: Oxford University Press, 1985), p. 523.

cision" is to do everything within your power to see that the president is fully briefed before he does make a decision. It's very important for the "oh, by the way" decision not to get made, because nine times out of ten the "oh, by the way" comment or recommendation is going to be coming off the wall, without being counterbalanced by a lot of other people who have something different to say about it.

Let me mention one thing. You just can't, given the president's constant exposure to the media, you can't protect him, no matter how carefully you try. In the early part of 1980, thousands upon thousands of Cuban refugees from Mariel Harbor in Cuba started crossing the Florida Straits. It was a problem of immense proportion. We were getting five thousand a day for a period.

It was a delicate situation because the refugees were breaking the law; they were illegal immigrants. At the same time, counterbalancing that, these people—men, women, and children, old people and quite young people, infants and helpless people, by and large—were in very small, dangerous boats. To them we had a humanitarian duty.

The president gave a speech in Washington, just one of those run-of-the-mill noonday speeches, and after the speech was over, someone from the press asked him what his attitude about the Mariel boatlift was. It was early in the boatlift. I had cautioned him about saying anything which would give any indication of U.S. approval, but he said something to the general effect that we had a humanitarian duty, we could not let these people die in the ninety miles between Cuba and here, and while they were breaking the law, nevertheless, our government would do everything we could to save their lives.

That caused tremendous problems because it was interpreted both by the Cubans, the American Cuban community in Florida, principally, and by a lot of the people in Cuba as being an open-door policy, "Come ahead." It ended up with our having about 130,000 illegal immigrants cross those Florida Straits.

So that there's no way that you can protect fully against the offhand remark, and an offhand remark by the president of the United States frequently can have implications or reverberations of a major decision, as I think that one did.

Chancellor: Mr. Sorensen, did you ever go in to President Kennedy and say, "This idea that you are circulating is a bad one"?

Theodore Sorensen: Let me first say that I'm here under false pretenses. I was not the White House chief of staff. Jack Kennedy was his own chief of staff.

Chancellor: I knew one of them would say that within the first fifteen minutes. (*Laughter*)

Sorensen: That's because we had a small enough staff that he could serve in that role. He was from time to time coming up with damn fool ideas, like going to the moon, for example.[5] (*Laughter*)

---

5. On May 25, 1961, President Kennedy appeared before a nationally televised joint session of Congress to appeal for approval of new programs that would put a man on the moon before the end of the decade. This goal, of course, was realized in July 1969.

There was a short way and a long way of handling ideas that I thought were mistaken. The long way has already been described here. I would say, "Well, let's staff that out, let's get a meeting on it," and I would make sure the people at the meeting were all against the idea. (*Laughter*)

The short way was to say "That sounds like something Dick Nixon would have suggested." (*Laughter*)

Chancellor: General Haig, how about you? You've got broad experience as a big forceful military man. Could you just march in? How do you feel when you go in to the president, and you know you are right, you know he's wrong. What goes through your mind? "Am I going to get fired?" What happens?

General Alexander Haig: What I usually did was to say, "Right, boss. I wish I had thought of that," and then go back and be sure he had time to think about it. I think that's the most important thing you can do, to protect him from some of these bumptious ideas that presidents get because they do have to, as Bob has said, have people around them who give them an opportunity to let off tensions and steam and protect them from themselves, so to speak.

But you must know your customer. Having been exposed to several chief executives under differing circumstances, I think sometimes it's best to say, "No, you are wrong." Other times, it's far better to say, "Well, let's think about it" or "Let's get some staff opinion on it." That's what is at the heart of the success of each and every one of the people who has had these responsibilities: to know their boss and to adjust to his idiosyncrasies.

Haldeman: And Haig and I didn't have the opportunity that Ted had to say, "That sounds like a Nixon idea." (*Laughter*)

Rumsfeld: The other side of the coin is that the president might be right and he's the president, and so the beauty is in the eye of the beholder. The chief of staff may think that it's a damn fool idea but, in fact, it may not be. In the last analysis, you have only one president, and I wouldn't want this little discussion to end by leaving the impression that a chief of staff actively subverted what the president wanted to do on his own hook because I didn't, and I'm sure no one in this room did.

In the last analysis, the president is the president and he is perfectly capable of taking your advice when you think he's wrong and staffing it with other people and even disagreeing with all of them, and going ahead and having it be right. It's not an accident that he's president and you are chief of staff. (*Laughter*)

Goodpaster: We had something that crystallized that pretty well. We called it Jack Martin's Empirical Rule Number One, and Jack took a while to reach this view.[6]

He had served on the staff of Senator Taft, and when Eisenhower became president, he asked Taft if he would send one of his staff people to work with Eisenhower so that he would be sure to understand

---

6. Jack Martin served as an administrative assistant to President Eisenhower from 1954 to 1958.

that point of view. He didn't always follow that point of view, and Jack was somewhat distressed by this for quite a while until he reflected on it. Just as Don said, when the president has thought it over and it's not a hasty action, and finally comes down on a position, then that is to be respected. Jack crystallized that in a short statement. His Empirical Rule Number One reads: "The president is right." (*Laughter*)

"Let's not make our mistakes in a hurry"

Chancellor: I'd like to ask you all now to move on to something that is more serious: crisis management. All of you have been there at the center of the storm when either domestic or international crises have come. In reading your biographies, I found a wide range of moments when your stomachs must have churned, when you must have been scared. Here you think of Sorensen and the Cuban Missile Crisis, among other things.

Let's begin by talking about the degree of involvement of the president when one of these crises starts, because sometimes it starts on a fairly low level. The other day the Iranian navy stopped an American ship near the Persian Gulf and boarded it in what apparently turned out to be a legal maneuver. The White House said that President Reagan was awakened at 2:00 o'clock in the morning and given the news.

Don, let me start with you. Is that a good way to

operate, to bring the president in at 2:00 in the morning and get him involved up front?

Rumsfeld: It's a judgment call, and it's not easy. Partly, it depends on the president. There's always the question, Are you better off getting your facts arranged, getting a little more information, and then bringing him in when a little bit of discipline has been put into the crisis or the issue, or is it better to bring him in early, let him begin to get comfortable with the evolution of the crisis? It's always a series of very tough calls.

Chancellor: Let me ask Dick Cheney, just theoretically, no particular president now: Is it wrong to bring the weight of the man, of the office itself, into some of these crises too early when the press picks it up, and suddenly the president has to say, "I think we have got to be humanitarian about these refugees," when maybe silence would be better? What are your thoughts on that?

Cheney: I think you're right, John. I think there's a tendency—at least our experience was, thinking back on it now—that oftentimes when these crises develop, that you end up sucking decisions into the White House that perhaps ought to be made someplace else.

Haig: The most important thing, I think, is the evolution of technology and its impact on crisis management. I think at the Gulf of Tonkin, President Johnson was engaged much too early, when we had just very fuzzy intelligence reports.[7]

---

7. In response to an encounter with North Vietnamese torpedo boats on August 2, 1964, the U.S. Navy ordered the *Maddox* to resume

The problem is twofold. It's not only in terms of intelligence; the fact that the president is exposed instantaneously through modern technology, satellite, with data that the other echelons below him are not getting, and wants answers and must have them. And he must have them because modern technology also brings the American public immediately abreast of the crisis, whether it's a terrorist act in West Beirut or whatever it may be, and presidents simply have to have answers. This has complicated the crisis-management process and, I think, endangered the ability to make rational decisions in time of stress.

Chancellor: I'd like you to go back to what Congressman Cheney was saying. Aren't there crises that are class C, class B, as well as big class A crises, and getting the president involved tends to escalate it? Any thoughts on that?

Cheney: It does, and the one power the president has, probably that's more important than maybe any other power, is his ability to set the national agenda,

---

operations in the Gulf of Tonkin. On the night of August 4, the *Maddox* and the *C. Turner Joy* reported they were under attack. Although there had been no visible sightings, and the heavy seas caused unreliable sonar reports, Johnson authorized retaliatory strikes against North Vietnamese torpedo boat bases and oil storage dumps. On August 7 the U.S. Congress passed the Gulf of Tonkin Resolution, which gave the president the power to use all measures necessary to "repel any armed attack" and "prevent further aggression" against U.S. forces. In the absence of a declaration of war, President Johnson, and subsequently President Nixon, enlisted the resolution to justify escalation of U.S. military involvement in South Vietnam. Congress repealed the resolution in 1970. George C. Herring, *America's Longest War: The United States and Vietnam, 1950–1975* (New York: Wiley, 1979), pp. 122–23.

to decide what is important by focusing on it, by talking about it, by focusing the attention of the press corps on it.

When you bring something to the presidential level, it automatically will—take something like the *Mayaguez* crisis, for example, one I'm familiar with.[8] All of a sudden, the president, his administration, is evaluated in terms of how he deals with that, although in the broad scheme of things, it's relatively insignificant compared to how you manage the economy or how you deal with your defense budget long-term.

But as Al says, the technology now makes it possible for the president to make a decision in a case involving military force that really ought to be made maybe by the commander of the aircraft carrier in the Tonkin Gulf or, in the case of the *Mayaguez*, off Cambodia, and the decision actually goes all the way up the chain, not only to CINCPAC [Commander-in-chief, Pacific] in Hawaii and the secretary of defense and the NSC [National Security Council] but ultimately ends up on the president's desk, and he makes

---

8. On May 12, 1975, the Khmer Rouge government of Cambodia fired on the U.S. merchant ship *Mayaguez* and forced it into the port of Sihanoukville. President Ford immediately convened the National Security Council and subsequently decided to capture the ship by force. On May 14, an hour before the Cambodian government planned to release the crew, U.S. military planes raided the Cambodian coast while marine units captured the vacant *Mayaguez*. The release of the thirty-nine-man crew proceeded, but the raid continued until the crew had boarded a U.S. naval vessel. Fifteen U.S. servicemen died in the fighting; another twenty-three were killed in a helicopter accident. The decisive nature of the operation was popular with the American people and evoked hearty public support for the president.

a relatively small decision that can have an enormous impact upon how he's perceived, and really should have been done by somebody else.

Haldeman: John? I think for this question and the general discussion, it's worth looking at the point you made, Isn't there a danger of escalating it by involving the president? That's an outsider's viewpoint. What we are talking about here with this group is really from the inside viewpoint. You aren't necessarily escalating something by bringing it to the president's attention *internally*, without involving the press and the world in the fact of the president's involvement. There can be a real value to the president's ongoing knowledge of the development of a crisis—but without the president running out and making a statement about it or issuing anything through a spokesman even, but simply keeping him involved as the thing progresses.

It depends on the nature of the crisis, as you were saying, the A, B, and C crises. You can make your A, B, and C classification on a lot of different bases. One of them is the immediacy basis. Some crises can't be resolved for a while and can't even be considered, even though you know they've happened. When the North Koreans shot down a plane early in our administration, we knew the plane was shot down but that was *all* we knew at that instant.[9] There wasn't any-

---

9. On April 15, 1969, North Korea shot down an American Navy EC-121 reconnaissance plane during a routine mission. Nixon, opting to continue the reconnaissance missions, decided against retaliation. See Nixon, *Memoirs*, pp. 382–84.

thing you could do about it then, but you had to start developing a plan for what you were going to do, and it was terribly important what that was, right from the earliest reaction. Therefore you brought the president in at the right time, but you didn't necessarily show the world that he was involved until he was ready to take a presidential position on it.

Sorensen: Much depends on the nature of the president and his philosophy of the presidency. One of his most important decisions is when *not* to decide or when *not* to get involved. There is no appeal on the president, so to speak, so his decision is likely to be a final one, unlike one at a lower level.

On the other hand, presidents also sometimes reach out for decisions that they don't have to reach out for because they deliberately want to be involved. President Kennedy remarked often that he was damned if the question of war with the Soviet Union over Berlin was going to be decided by some sergeant on the border making a decision with respect to a tank or a troop movement. He personally monitored the conduct of our armed forces during the Cuban Missile Crisis, and it turned out it was a good thing he did because he and the chief of naval operations had a very fundamental difference, one on which a war might have hung in the balance.[10]

---

10. The United States imposed a naval blockade (euphemistically labeled a "quarantine") around Cuba on October 22, 1962. In order to allow the Soviets maximum time to evaluate their options, Kennedy ordered that the quarantine line be drawn much closer to Cuban shores than the Navy commanders preferred. According to

Watson: We have a tendency generally to think only in terms of international crises, the *Mayaguez* or the Cuban crises. In March 1979 the Three Mile Island matter occurred. That was a situation in which, to illustrate Ted's point just now, there was a terrible and unknown consequence which we were having great difficulty gauging.[11] We didn't want to get the president out front and involved because we thought that the president's speaking about that and being personally involved in it would escalate the matter beyond where our knowledge would permit us to go. So while we were keeping him informed internally at every turn of the day, he was not, either through a spokesman or otherwise, actively taking much of a role or saying much about it.

That was an interesting situation in which at the time I was not the chief of staff. I was secretary to the cabinet and I was, and had been for a couple of years, the president's crisis manager for domestic crises of

---

Graham Allison's account, Chief of Naval Operations George Anderson resisted the president's order by positioning U.S. ships much farther out, thereby hastening the moment of their confrontation with incoming Soviet ships. As a result, Kennedy was forced to allow one or more Soviet ships to pass through the blockade after it had been officially imposed. Allison, *Essence of Decision: Explaining the Cuban Missile Crisis* (Boston: Little, Brown, 1971), pp. 128–32.

11. A series of breakdowns in the cooling system of the Three Mile Island nuclear plant reactor led to a major accident on March 28, 1979. The Nuclear Regulatory Commission was initially unsure of the severity of the accident's consequences. On March 30 it warned of a possible core meltdown or explosion. Five days after the accident, President Carter visited the site in an effort to demonstrate that radiation levels near Three Mile Island were not hazardous.

whatever nature. I got a call from the governor of Pennsylvania, Dick Thornburgh, who said to me, "Something terrible, it looks like, has happened at Three Mile Island, the nuclear power plant. I'm getting conflicting information and don't know exactly what to do."

I contacted the Nuclear Regulatory Commission. We started to find out exactly what was going on and then immediately put somebody there. That was a situation in which I informed the president immediately, even before I had much information about it, because the stakes were so high. We were considering in the early moments, in fact, in the early days of that crisis, a national catastrophe which could have involved a half-million lives being lost.

Rumsfeld: John, you mentioned the A, B, and C crises. That's very easy to do after the fact. It is not very easy to do at the time.

What you worry about in the international crisis is escalation, and a military or political action that is executed because of a lack of information about the developing crisis can, in fact, be a political signal that might be exactly one you don't want to send. So you have the problem, a very great risk of failing to inform, in some instances, during a process of escalation because you could give a signal that would be totally harmful to you.

McPherson: Could I make a wild generalization at this point, an unfounded generalization about presidents? I'm taking up Ted Sorensen's notion that all this depends very much on what kind of a fellow there is in the White House. Years ago someone told me that presidents were two things, a chief of state and a chief of government. He said it had been his observation that the chiefs of state did fine over the long haul with the public. They were the guys up on the bridge of the ship who saw the big picture and sailed ahead with their capes flowing in the wind. Remember that wonderful World War II picture of Roosevelt with his cape up there, looking very much the leader, the chief of state.

But the chief of government is the guy who loves to go down to the engine room with his hammer and his wrench and bang around and work on things and work on whether this guy ought to be promoted to that position or that fellow ought to be fired.

Sorensen: Or who plays on the White House tennis court.[12]

McPherson: Or who plays on the White House tennis court. That was a great crisis decision of our times. (*Laughter*)

It seems to me that in our period here, the twenty-five-year period we are talking about here, chiefs of state who have done particularly well, if you take that up-on-the-bridge, long-view idea of a chief of state, are Eisenhower and Reagan. President Reagan—I don't mean this in any pernicious way, but he

---

12. A common criticism of Jimmy Carter's management style was his insistence on giving personal attention to routine decisions that should have been resolved at a lower level. Carter's personal adjudication of a dispute among staff over tennis court access and schedules is perhaps the most widely cited example of the extremes to which this president assumed the "burdens of office."

slept through the Gulf of Sidra crisis.[13] Nobody woke
him up. It wasn't his fault; he was asleep. But Mr.
Meese didn't wake him up because he didn't see any
need to while that was going on.

Well, President Johnson, if that had happened and
he hadn't been waked up, I don't know what he—
wouldn't have done him any good to have been
waked up, but he would have been furious not to have
been called. He said he was sure he wanted to be
called every time something happened in the Vietnam War era. He said, "I'm sure that someday, my
luck being what it is, a guy is going to call me from
the National Security Council staff at 3:00 in the
morning and tell me that a navy pilot has dropped a
bomb down the smokestack of a Russian freighter sitting in Hanoi Harbor. And *that* navy pilot would have
been born and raised in Johnson City, Texas." (*Laughter*) He really wanted to know the particulars.

And my generalization is that perhaps Democratic
presidents, being more government-oriented, being
more oriented toward the use of government than the
Republican presidents we have had in the last
twenty-five years, that is, shaping government, starting these big programs that everybody sooner or
later wrings their hands over and so on—Democrats
are likely to be involved. They are likely to be wanting to get their hands of the throttles, whereas the
successful Republican presidents in the polls, Eisenhower and Reagan, particularly, have been much

---

13. In August 1981 in an air battle sixty miles off the Libyan coast
    above the northern Gulf of Sidra, U.S. navy jets downed two Lib-
    yan aircraft.

more inclined to sit back and let the staff deal with it until some moment at which they can speak, rather, from the mountaintop.

Goodpaster: This relates to that a bit, but it's a different kind of a crisis. I'm going back to when the Russians put up *Sputnik* in 1957. Now, we had known that satellites were under preparation. We had one that we intended to put up as part of the International Geophysical Year. It was being done under scientific direction and without a great sense of urgency to it. When *Sputnik* went up, the president's initial reaction was, "Well, all right. They put one up a little ahead of ours. No big thing." There was some comment about cosmic basketball games or something the size of a grapefruit, not all that important.

That lasted about thirty-six hours, and then you began to sense that, somehow, the confidence of the American people had been shaken, and at that point, President Eisenhower decided it was time for him to get into this. He called together the scientific group, as I recall, Professor Rabi and Jim Killian came down.[14] He then established a scientific advisory

---

14. The launching of *Sputnik* on October 4, 1957, shocked many Americans: It suddenly appeared that the Soviets had passed the U.S. in technological leadership. In addition to its propaganda value, the launch proved that the Soviets had developed the world's most powerful rocket booster, the prerequisite for an intercontinental ballistic missile that could reach the U.S. The immediate public panic eventually resulted in a massive effort to upgrade the nation's educational system, build up military defenses, and regain the lead in the race for space. To help calm the uproar, Eisenhower created the post of special assistant to the president for science

committee and he then began to display a set of actions that would restore the confidence of the people that indeed, we were not going to be caught short.

McPherson: Not before we Democrats had a lot of fun with that basketball game. (*Laughter*)

Goodpaster: I remember it. It took about thirty-six hours, as I say, but about the second or third swipe of that two-by-four, we began to understand what was involved in this thing.

Chancellor: Harry McPherson, let me go back to you just for a minute. Talking about the president who likes to get down into the workings of government and all that presents you with the familiar image of Lyndon Johnson ordering bombing targets in Vietnam and getting involved in all kinds of very detailed orders to the people who were prosecuting the war on the ground. When you look back on that now, Harry, was that a bad thing for him, to have been that involved?

McPherson: I'm not sure he really was as much involved as that image would suggest. He was far more involved, for example, in the domestic crises of our time.

You know, if anybody had practice in crisis management, it was Johnson and his staff because we had

---

and technology and appointed James Killian, then president of MIT, to that post. Eisenhower also enlisted the aid of Isidor Rabi, a noted scientist who had worked on the Manhattan Project and advised the Atomic Energy Commission.

both Vietnam and the riots in the cities.[15] I can't really speak for the bombing target selection and Johnson's role in it as much as I can speak of his role as president and political leader at a time when his cities were burning up, were suddenly exploding in all directions. In that situation, it was absolutely essential that he become and stay involved, that he be on the phone with the mayors and the governors and the black leaders, with the FBI, with the, sadly, generals of the army who were running the Eighty-second Airborne or something of that kind. Remember those days? Sending people, sending troops into Detroit and Chicago, and other cities. That was something that so much involved the political structure and sanity of the country that the president had to be involved at every moment.

I don't know whether President Johnson was overly involved in the specific tactical decisions of Vietnam. I don't know, but my sense is that he was nowhere near as involved as, say, Roosevelt was in World War II. I can't speak for Truman.

Haig: Let me raise the example of the Gulf of Tonkin. No one around the president is going to shield him from urgent intelligence that comes in from global intelligence capabilities. President Johnson was led to believe that we had a destroyer under North Vietnamese attack. He ordered Bob McNamara, for whom I worked at the time—he was then secretary

---

15. During a week of disorders in the Watts district of Los Angeles in August 1965, thirty-four people died; in July 1967 riots left forty dead in Detroit and twenty-six dead in Newark. All three riots were precipitated by altercations between blacks and local police.

of defense—to launch counteractions. The president asked the chairman of the Joint Chiefs of Staff and Bob McNamara, "How long will it take you to conduct these actions?" Their judgment was four, five hours. Well, I recall that night very well. At 6:00 o'-clock, Mr. Johnson had scheduled a television broadcast to the nation and the order hadn't even gotten out of the Pentagon to the fleet in the Pacific to conduct that strike. It was a very, very difficult three or four hours until finally, the president gave the speech before the bombs hit the target. This is the kind of thing that can happen as a consequence of modern technology, and it is important for those who are delivering information to the chief executive to know that the people in the field who are going to have to execute crisis management don't even have the benefit of that information.

Goodpaster: That's a very good point. Eisenhower had a saying that he used a number of times. He said, "Now, boys, let's not make our mistakes in a hurry." (*Laughter*)

One of the great moments, going back to the initial question, was when he would propose something and be a little assertive and anxious to get on with it. I recall on occasion telling him, "Mr. President, I've heard a wonderful saying, I don't recall where it came from, but 'Let's not make our mistakes in a hurry.' " And he would take that well.

Sorensen: I think that everyone up here could testify to one important lesson a president learns about crisis management in the course of his presidency, and that is who should be in the room.

Our first crisis involving Cuba was the Bay of Pigs,

and that was a fiasco handled badly from beginning to end. The president, regarding that crisis, met with a very small group because of their office. He hardly knew them, having just begun the presidency. Communication was bad; turned out the advice and the planning were bad.[16]

Our second Cuban crisis, the Cuban Missile Crisis, the only people in that room were those whom John F. Kennedy wanted to be there because he had confidence in their judgment. There were all different kinds of ranks in that room. There were people from a certain level in a certain department but not other people from a higher level in that department. Those were the ones whom he wanted, and that worked out much better.

Chancellor: Wasn't there a point at which someone asked the president to leave the Excom meetings because

---

16. After his election, Kennedy learned that the CIA had been training an exile group in Guatemala for an eventual invasion of Cuba. With misgivings, the new president approved the plan. On April 17, 1961, some fifteen hundred exiles landed at the Bay of Pigs and were pinned down on the beaches by Fidel Castro's forces. Due to a delay in U.S. air support and the failure of an anticipated uprising among the Cuban populace, the invaders were defeated in two days—a stunning blow to the U.S. and to Kennedy, who took full responsibility for the debacle. For an insider's account, see Theodore C. Sorensen, *Kennedy* (New York: Harper & Row, 1965), pp. 291–309.

Richard E. Neustadt reviews this sequence of mishaps in exploring the risks of presidential transition: "In this Bay of Pigs affair the new regime's decision-making showed two striking features, ignorance and hopefulness. The ignorance was tinged with innocence, the hopefulness with arrogance." Neustadt, *Presidential Power: The Politics of Leadership from FDR to Carter*, rev. ed. (New York: Wiley, 1980), pp. 220–23.

his presence there was inhibiting debate?[17] Am I right in that?

Sorensen: That is correct. We had a series of meetings all during that week, and the president felt it important to keep up his normal schedule so that there would be no leak to the Soviets that we were aware of the missiles in Cuba. When he came back from one of these meetings, having been away, Attorney General Robert Kennedy and I said to him, "To tell you the truth, in one sense, the meetings went very well without you. The subordinates are

---

17. Throughout the summer of 1962, U.S. intelligence monitored the Soviet military build-up in Cuba. On October 16 President Kennedy was informed that photoanalysis revealed the construction on the Cuban mainland of sites for nuclear-capable intermediate range ballistic missiles. Kennedy immediately convened a group of close advisors, dubbed the Excom (Executive Committee of the National Security Council), with Attorney General Robert Kennedy directing the deliberations. Committee members included Secretary of State Dean Rusk, Secretary of Defense Robert McNamara, CIA Director John McCone, Secretary of the Treasury C. Douglas Dillon, Special Assistant for National Security Affairs McGeorge Bundy, Special Counsel Theodore Sorensen, Deputy Secretary of State Alexis Johnson, Assistant Secretary of State Edwin Martin, Special Advisor on Soviet Affairs Llewellyn Thompson, Assistant Secretary of Defense Paul Nitze, and Chairman of the Joint Chiefs of Staff Maxwell Taylor.

The group considered both military options, such as an invasion of Cuba or a surgical airstrike to destroy the missile sites, and diplomatic solutions, including an agreement whereby the U.S. would remove its Jupiter missiles from Turkey in exchange for a Soviet withdrawal from Cuba. The president settled on a compromise measure and imposed a naval blockade around Cuba on October 22, 1962. After several days of tense diplomatic maneuvering, Soviet Premier Nikita Khrushchev agreed to dismantle the missile sites in return for U.S. pledges neither to invade nor to use force to topple Castro's government.

more willing to contradict their superiors when you are not there. An undersecretary of state or assistant secretary of state will never contradict the secretary in front of you, but they did it very frankly when you were gone." The president said, "I think I'll stay away from some more meetings."

Chancellor: Was that true of Nixon? Were there times when you would try to get very senior people in who could yell at each other because the president wasn't there?

Haldeman: Yes, but we didn't have to. Nixon wanted it done that way, and he purposely set up, as we did, for domestic or international situations, an adversarial proceeding within the staff. We always, on a major decision, had differing points of view brought together out of those discussions and differing alternatives presented to the president that would give him a range of options, always with a recommendation but not necessarily a consensus recommendation. Often, not a consensus recommendation. As everybody here constantly says, the president does make the decision.

But in that process of finding out where you are and where you can go, there is some real value to working things out at the staff level without the president involved, for exactly the reasons Ted said. Within the bureaucracy and the military structure and so on, you are not going to have low-level people contradicting higher-level people in front of the highest level. So that kind of interchange did take place, but our system basically was designed that way. It was routinely done, not a thing that we had to do from time to time.

Chancellor: Or "ad hoc'd," as they sometimes say in the White House.

Access and secrecy, intelligence and dumb luck

Chancellor: Jack Watson, can there be too much secrecy? I'm really thinking of the Desert One hostage rescue operation, which was so carefully held and yet the Carter administration, trying to rescue the hostages in Teheran, had to get involved with the marines and the navy and the army and the air force and all that.[18]

---

18. On November 4, 1979, soon after the deposed shah of Iran had been admitted to the U.S. for medical treatment, the U.S. embassy in Teheran was stormed and sixty-three Americans were taken hostage. After releasing ten female and black hostages, the revolutionary council of Ayatollah Khomeini refused to negotiate, and securing the release of the remaining Americans came to dominate the administration of Jimmy Carter. With the repeated failure of economic and political sanctions, on April 11, 1980, Carter convened the National Security Council to deliberate a military rescue mission. Secretary of State Cyrus Vance did not attend but throughout had strongly objected to military action. Persuaded by the arguments of National Security Advisor Zbigniew Brzezinski, Carter authorized a rescue attempt. On April 21, three days before the rescue, Vance privately submitted his resignation to the president. The mechanical failure of several helicopters in the Iranian desert forced the mission commander to abort the operation; eight Americans died in an accident during the withdrawal. Carter publicly accepted Vance's resignation on April 28, naming Senator Edmund Muskie to replace him. See Jimmy Carter, *Keeping Faith: Memoirs of a President* (New York: Bantam Books, 1982), pp. 506–22; Cyrus Vance, *Hard Choices: Critical Years in America's Foreign Policy* (New York: Simon & Schuster, 1983). For a chief of staff's

What are your thoughts now that you look back on that sadly unsuccessful mission? Was there too much secrecy? Was there not enough of the kind of consultation that Bob Haldeman and others were talking about?

Watson: No, I think that that is a classic illustration, in my own judgment, of where secrecy of the most absolute sort was necessary. As everyone knows, that was a high-risk situation of the first magnitude. It was logistically and militarily a superhuman effort. We had to transport those helicopters a very long distance from the carriers, over desert under cover of night. It was a highly, highly risky thing.

We kept it closed because any kind of leakage, any kind of intimation to the enemy, to, in this case, the Iranians, that we were even contemplating some assault, some initiative, would have made a very high-risk situation literally impossible. It's my opinion that there are situations, that mission being a classic example, where you must maintain secrecy. No one in the White House knew except those who absolutely had to know. In government and military parlance, there are those who *need to know* and those for whom it would be nice to know certain things. That was a need-to-know situation, and I think the fact that we were able to keep it a secret as we did is attributable to the people who were involved. There were absolutely no leaks.

With respect to the consultation, John, it was a

---

perspective, see Hamilton Jordan, *Crisis: The Last Year of the Carter Presidency* (New York: Putnam, 1982).

tragic affair, but it was not a tragic affair because people had not spoken their minds. There was, in fact, a difference of opinion, of which the president was keenly aware, as to whether or not that rescue mission should have even taken place. It was not because his key need-to-know advisors had not had a full and fair, unrestrained opportunity to tell him what they thought. He ultimately simply had to make a command judgment about whether the risk should be taken.

Chancellor: And you lost a secretary of state when Cyrus Vance resigned.

Watson: Precisely so.

Haldeman: On this need-to-know issue that Jack's raising, I don't mean to imply that we had a broad range of people involved in everything, either. There were a number of major crises or major decisions, at least, such as the whole opening of China initiative, the invasion of Cambodia, incursion into Cambodia, the bombing of Hanoi—there were a number of major decisions that were made with very, very limited groups of people, the selective process that Ted talks about, people who had to be involved in that decision. But no matter how small the group, there was always the effort to have the balance and sometimes to test.

We had one major decision which related to the Hanoi bombing activity and mining of Haiphong. That was believed to be in danger of impinging upon the president's planned visit to the Soviet Union. There was a substantial difference within the very highest levels of the president's advisors, and this was a totally secret activity.[19]

Chancellor: The mining was, what, four weeks before the visit? Everybody was writing, everybody must have been telling you, "Well, the Russians will disinvite him."

Haldeman: Yes. In the infinite wisdom of the press commentators—you weren't a commentator at that time, John—the infinite wisdom was that the president had done a stupid thing and hadn't even thought about the fact that the mining might impinge upon the Soviet trip, which, of course, was the overriding consideration that had been—

Haig: Well, this is a case of "how do you prevent presidents from doing crazy things?"

Haldeman: That's right.

Haig: And only one or two people told President Nixon that the Russians wanted the summit so badly that they would go ahead regardless of what he did. That was the lesson we all should have absorbed at the time anyway. So it was his decision against a very

---

19. Renewed U.S. military activity in North Vietnamese territory came in response to Hanoi's major offensive in the south in March 1972, an action President Nixon viewed as Hanoi's attempt to capitalize on continuing U.S. troop withdrawals. Nixon authorized the first U.S. air attacks deep inside the north since 1969 and ordered the mining of Haiphong Harbor—a step Lyndon Johnson had considered and rejected in order to avoid sinking Soviet or Chinese ships. Despite these actions, the Moscow summit took place as scheduled. See Nixon, *Memoirs*, p. 607.

time anyway. So it was his decision against a very strong consensus not to put the summit in jeopardy that I think ultimately brought that war to a conclusion, which we ultimately—

Chancellor: You know something that I have learned now that I'm a commentator?

Haldeman: And have acquired infinite wisdom.

Chancellor: And have acquired infinite wisdom. When you are writing about presidents, never write that they are as dumb as they often seem.

Haldeman: Right. That's very sound advice to your colleagues. (*Laughter*)

Chancellor: Let me ask you about things that happen, Mr. Haldeman. Let's take the bombing of Cambodia. The United States bombed Cambodia. The Cambodians who were being bombed knew it. Prince Sihanouk and the other Cambodians knew it. The Russians knew it. But the White House wouldn't tell the American people that it was going on. Are there dynamics within certain decisions that require, even if the rest of the world knows, that you can't tell the Americans?

Haldeman: The rest of the world *didn't* know. A part of the world *did* know, and Al can speak more directly to this. The first activity that Al Haig and I really had together was some secret meetings on an airplane in an airport in a foreign country going into exactly that question. That was the "Menu Operation," wasn't it? Breakfast and lunch and so on?

Haig: Right.

Chancellor: Code words.

Haldeman: That's right.

Haig: And indigestion.

Haldeman: And indigestion, yes, that was the primary one. (*Laughter*)

The whole problem of the pursuit of the Vietnam War, in our administration, trying to pick up from something that was well underway long before we got there, was based on the intent to negotiate a treaty to end the war. The negotiations had to be conducted in secret, and neither the American people nor anybody else knew precisely what was going on.

One of my early moments of losing my passion for the anonymity that was supposed to be the qualification of a senior White House advisor was when I went on a television broadcast at the president's orders and made the statement at the president's orders, which wasn't known at the time, that those who were criticizing some actions we were taking—those in the Senate who were criticizing some actions we were taking in Vietnam at the time—were consciously aiding and abetting the enemy. I made that statement.

Chancellor: Pretty tough language.

Haldeman: Yes, it was viewed that way by some of the senators who took it fairly personally. (*Laughter*)

Chancellor: Isn't that part of the Treason Act?

Haldeman: Those happen to be the same words that are in the Treason Act. But the point was that what they were saying, consciously saying, was very clearly aiding and abetting the enemy because what they didn't know was that what they were demanding we do was substantially less than what we were already doing at the conference table, at the treaty bargaining table. But that couldn't be discussed.

Some responsible senators on the other side, on the Democratic side of the Senate, were very much aware of what we were doing because the president did keep the Democratic leadership informed. But there were other senators, for their own purposes, who were playing the critique game, and in the process, undermining—Al bore the brunt of this because the gentleman, who won't be named, for whom he worked at the time became highly distressed about the fact that his negotiations were being shot down by the United States Senate.[20]

Chancellor: That was the unnamed official who spoke with the German accent.

Haldeman: That's the one. Right. (*Laughter*)

Haig: I think the point you're making, John, is: Are there things that presidents *must* keep secret? And the answer to that is: of course. One of the greatest examples in the Nixon administration was the initiative

---

20. This unnamed "gentleman" is, of course, Henry Kissinger, who served in the White House as special advisor on national security from 1969 to 1976. While retaining his White House position, Kissinger succeeded William P. Rogers as secretary of state in 1973. He retained these dual responsibilities throughout Nixon's tenure but left his White House staff position late in President Ford's term.

toward the People's Republic of China. Had the president shared with the Congress and the American people the fact that a dialogue had begun, a very tentative one, with Beijing, I can assure you the opposition on the Hill would have been so vehement that there never would have been an opening to the People's Republic of China. So indeed, there are times when presidents must abide by secrecy, not just in conflict situations but in diplomacy as well.

Rumsfeld: Wasn't it Winston Churchill, talking about the Normandy invasion, the date and the location, who said, "Sometimes the truth is so precious, it must be accompanied by a bodyguard of lies"?

Chancellor: Let's go back to the operation of the White House, and let me talk to you, Mr. Rumsfeld, because you were there in 1975 when the *Mayaguez* was seized, an American ship on the high seas seized by the Cambodians, or by some Cambodians. Now, Harry McPherson, you were in the Johnson White House when the North Koreans seized an American ship, the *Pueblo*. The *Pueblo* was seized by them, you remember, and it dragged on forever. It was an unresolved and painful episode for the Johnson administration.[21]

---

21. On January 23, 1968, the U.S. intelligence ship *Pueblo* was seized in international waters off the coast of North Korea. One American was killed, eighty-two were taken hostage. To secure the release of the crew, the U.S. signed a bogus admission of espionage activities within North Korea's territorial waters, a statement the U.S. government promptly repudiated once the hostages were freed on December 22, 1968.

Was that experience in your mind when you people were dealing with the *Mayaguez*?

Rumsfeld: There's no question but that there was a deep concern on the part of the secretary of state and secretary of defense, and the National Security Council, that once the crew of that ship were taken ashore, that the problem would be fifty times more difficult.

Chancellor: But was the *Pueblo* in your mind?

Rumsfeld: No question. Clearly, the *Pueblo* was taken at sea, escorted in, and the crew were in fact brought into North Korea. There was a concern in the White House that if the crew were taken off the island or the *Mayaguez*, the ship itself, and put on the mainland, that in fact, the problem would be vastly more difficult. The *Pueblo* experience was very much in people's minds, and it also put a time problem in front of you that was different from something like the Iranian hostage rescue, where you controlled the time.

Chancellor: How about the technology? How about your intelligence? Was it any good?

Rumsfeld: It's funny. It comes in pieces. It's incomplete; it's inadequate. You never know if it is complete or not, and it comes dribbling in, and then you try to find out more. In this case, it came through a civilian merchant shipping line that heard some radio call. That was the first news and, of course, it was a part of the world where we have very few military assets. It was a very difficult situation.

Now, you asked about technology. In fact, there was a time when the president of the United States

was in the Cabinet Room—Dick, correct me if I'm
wrong.

Cheney: You're entirely correct.

Rumsfeld: —with the National Security Council, and he
was receiving reports from the next room that were
the actual words of the pilot who was flying over the
Mayaguez and over the straits and over a boat that
was taking people from the island to the mainland.
The pilot was talking, and it was being repeated to
the president in real time. The pilot was flying low
over this. He was some, you know, twenty-three-year-
old guy.

Chancellor: Slow down. This is a marvelous story. The
president was in the Cabinet Room, and did they
have this on a speaker in another room?

Rumsfeld: My recollection is it was on a speaker in another room in the White House, probably in the Situation Room. Dick, do you recall?

Cheney: Yes, I think it was. He was sitting in the Cabinet
Room.

Rumsfeld: We were in the Cabinet Room.

Cheney: And in the room right next to it, the report was
coming in over the phone lines.

Rumsfeld: But the report was, in effect, from the pilot.
Now, here, you can imagine, here's the chain of command: the president, the secretary of defense, the
unified specified commanders, and then some cap-
tain aboard a ship that's got airplanes, a squadron

commander, and then finally this little pilot. He's out there flying around.

And he gets down over this boat that's chugging from the island to the mainland, and he says, "I see people on there." And the next thing you hear is him saying, "They look like Caucasians, and they are halfway to the shore." And then everyone looks at the president. (*Laughter*) He eventually is going to say to somebody, "Stop it, sink it, don't let them get there. Don't sink it. You'll kill them if it is. Are you sure?" It's goofy the way technology has put a president in that position.

Chancellor: Exactly right. That's what General Haig brought up.

Rumsfeld: Exactly.

Chancellor: Congressman Cheney, talk to us about that a little bit. If the president knows this, how many presidents are going to walk away from it saying, "It's time for my sauna, gentlemen, I will see you later"? (*Laughter*) They can't, can they? Once they hear that symbolic voice on the speaker, however it comes in, are they stuck?

Cheney: They are stuck. They have to make a decision. The other thing, I think, it also has a depressing effect upon the initiative of all those people in the organization between the president and that pilot out there over the ocean. You've got four-star generals and admirals and people who have spent their entire lives dealing with these kinds of forces, and all of a sudden, you've placed the emphasis upon them passing the buck up the chain.

Nobody is willing to take responsibility for making a decision that under other circumstances they would. But it ends up right smack on the president's desk, and he ultimately is going to have to make that decision about whether or not the pilot goes forward and sinks the boat. In this case, President Ford made the decision to let the boat proceed. Turned out to be the right decision, but it was basically just dumb luck.

Chancellor: Flip of the coin, though, wasn't it?

Cheney: It was a flip of the coin. It could have gone the other way. The pilot could have followed the instructions he'd received earlier, sunk the boat, and killed the entire crew.

McPherson: But he was very much on his own. If it had gone on a little bit longer and if more of the Defense Department had been involved, and then the State Department had been involved, State would have prepared papers on the nature of the Cambodian culture. (*Laughter*) The Defense Department would have said, "This can't possibly be done unless we get an increase in appropriations." (*Laughter*) And "NBC Nightly News" would have said, "We are very troubled about the way the president—" (*Laughter and applause*)

Chancellor: Mr. Haldeman, during the 1970s, wasn't there a big leap in our ability to have satellite technology, satellite pictures, satellite information coming into the White House? It's a general theme that I think is so terribly important, that technology has entered the White House in a way that is pushing the president.

Haldeman: Yes. The leap was in the 1960s, really. We had the super-satellite technology prior to our coming to the White House in '69.

Chancellor: What did it mean to have it? Without violating any confidences, were you getting photographs, or how does that work?

Sorensen: I'll give you the best example that they told us. You could tell whether a picnic table in the park in Moscow had a tablecloth on it or not.

Haldeman: It's very precise. (*Laughter*)

Chancellor: But how quickly does that get to you? Is that next-day mail or is that—

Haldeman: Same-day mail.

Haig: Some instances, it's the same day. But the first customer is the president.

This technology has affected the decision-making process in another very subtle way, and we see it today in terrorism and counter-terrorism. We began to downgrade human judgment, risk-taking by the greatest computer every devised, the human brain, and substitute for that the demand that a fact is not a fact unless you have a satellite photograph of that fact or an electronic intercept of that fact. That's what's constantly going on.

I think [Secretary of State] George Shultz two days ago commented that there are times when you must take action when you don't have this kind of evidentiary confirmation of a fact. But that's been one of the great tendencies, and that has distorted crisis management in our government, in my view.

Cheney: Let me add, too, that a key part of the whole intelligence operation isn't just collecting intelligence and getting good pictures. Somebody with a lot of know-how has to be able to sit down and analyze that intelligence and draw proper conclusions from it.

When you start to lay all that sophisticated information on the political staff in the White House, most of them, especially early in the administration, simply aren't equipped to deal with it. If you are relatively new, just through a presidential campaign, you're an expert in delegate selection in the Republican party, but you don't know the difference between the SS-25 and the SS-18 or whatever is coming into the pictures. There's a real tendency in those early crises—you get better at it over time, everybody has—but there's a real tendency in those first ones to provide information to people who really aren't equipped to evaluate it.

If one could rewrite the book . . .

Chancellor: We are going to change the subject now from the crisis management that the White House exercises when things go wrong to how things go more generally. How do you run the place?

Congressman Cheney, you worked for President Ford. If you had to do it again, how would you do it differently?

Cheney: First of all, I would have begun his term in office with his election rather than his inheriting the office.

Chancellor: That's important.

Cheney: Important point, because we were so constrained by the circumstances, by the way we came to power. That really placed limits on us that were with us throughout in terms of whom we could hire and whom we could keep and all those kinds of issues and questions. The other thing I would do, I think, would be to try to persuade the president to be even tougher on personnel than he was.

As I look back on it, there were times when we had major problems internally in terms of trying to manage the place. It's a problem for every chief of staff. You wind up with people who, frankly, shouldn't be there, egos get in the way, and relationships are such that frankly, there are people who need to be fired.

Chancellor: Old pals?

Cheney: Old pals oftentimes, sometimes new pals. The criticism is often made of chiefs of staff for having been brutal in firing personnel. But somebody has to do it. The chief of staff is the one who inherits that responsibility. If I were to look back at the Ford years, there are some people I wished I had fired. (*Laughter*)

Chancellor: But a cabinet member serves at the direction and the pleasure of the president. Yet you say if the cabinet member is going to be fired, the chief of staff has to do it? Doesn't the president have that responsibility?

Cheney: The president has to make the decision. You don't go out independently or wake up some morning and say, "Gee, I think I'll fire the secretary of defense today." You've got to go to the president. He may have initiated it, but if there's a dirty deed to be done, it's the chief of staff who's got to do it. The president gets credit for what works, and you get the blame for what doesn't work. That's the nature of the beast.

The only reason you are there is to serve the president of the United States, and one of the most difficult things he has to do is deal with unpleasant personnel decisions and situations. It goes with the turf. If you are not prepared to do that, then somebody else ought to have the job.

Chancellor: Dick the Knife. (*Laughter*) General Haig, what would you have done differently in the Nixon White House? You were there in a pretty tough time.

Haig: They were certainly not easy times. I'm not so sure I would have done a great deal differently. We had a peculiar set of circumstances where we had to bring in some new blood and some new credibility and some new political influence. With that come liabilities, too, but I think it was necessary, because at that point the president's credibility had been damaged, not fatally but substantially. From that point on, it was managing the institution of the presidency, the preservation of that institution and, I think, the rights of the incumbent.

We are not a banana republic, but there were tendencies for some on the Hill and many in the press to try to propel us into such a configuration. I think it would have been a disaster for the American people, for our Constitution, and our country.

You know, the institution of the presidency carries with it a very important policing mechanism for the American people. I served seven presidents, four at very close range, and each, in the evolution of his experience in the office, becomes more and more concerned as to how he is going to be viewed by history. Many of the human peccadilloes that are associated with their character, I find, have been sublimated to their overall concern about their place in history.

Chancellor: Harry McPherson, Johnson administration; lots of turmoil. If you could write the book again for that administration, what would you do differently?

McPherson: I came to the Johnson administration in February 1965, just a few months before the final decision was made to put enormous numbers of American troops into Vietnam. I had no role in those meetings. I was a young counsel to him, his special counsel, and was to become his speechwriter, and ultimately became involved in Vietnam.

What I would have done differently: I would have gone into a phone booth and taken off my suit and come out with my Superman suit on and would have gone into those meetings and said, "Either stay out, either withdraw the American advisors as rapidly as possible while you load up the South Vietnamese army as rapidly as possible, or invest a very large military force at once and try to win it." I suppose. I think of myself and of everybody who was around

President Johnson in those days as desperately trying to find the best way out of a tragic situation. Very much like Oedipus wishing he'd never met his father along the road.

There is a terrible, grinding inexorability to events. The same was true, I think, in the rioting in the cities. People who had been long suppressed, through a whole concatenation of political and demographic events, social events, great migrations from the South to the North—those events suddenly just occurred, and how does a president "ride that tiger," as President Kennedy used to say?

Chancellor: Do you think, Harry, that there was some other way? As this kind of gothic inevitability of involvement in Vietnam grew larger, as you were drawn into the "big muddy," could there have been any way of handling his presidency—the staff that advised him, the information that he was getting, the range of opinions that he would have—that might have not gotten us so involved in Vietnam?

McPherson: Yes, I suppose so. There were advisors— George Ball, perhaps, principal among them—urgently arguing that we should get out altogether because this was not our part of the world, Southeast Asia.[22]

The problem was a multiple one. It includes a

---

22. George W. Ball was named undersecretary of state for economic affairs in January 1961; in November he became undersecretary of state. He was an early and constant foe of American involvement in Vietnam; convinced that he could not change American policy, he left office in September 1966.

transformation of Lyndon Johnson's television persona into Ronald Reagan's. That would have helped a lot, to be a war leader instead of a Methodist bishop manqué.

Chancellor: Mr. Haldeman, you came into the White House in 1969. In serving the president, you set up a pretty tight ship in there with you at the top. Don't be offended by "tight ship," but people reported to you and you reported to the president. Looking back on it, was that system that you and President Nixon had in those first few years the way you would do it again if you could write the book?

Haldeman: I've got to correct the premise before I can deal with the conclusion. We set up a tight ship, admittedly, but it was not set up on the basis that people reported to me and I reported to the president. There were a number of assistants to the president who reported directly to the president. The cabinet officers reported directly to the president, and a number of agency heads reported directly to the president. Actually, way too many people. That's one of the problems with the office of the presidency that perhaps we will get into as we look toward what ought to be done.

The point of our system was to try to do this in an orderly way. It was not to circumvent any individual whom the president wanted reporting to him and who had a reason to report to him. It was to make it possible for them to do it in a way that gave them the time they needed with the president at the time they needed it. The system channeled and balanced and assured that opposing views would be coming in, avoiding the possibility of someone dominating the president on one issue from one direction and thereby filibustering out the opposing view.

Would he have done it differently? My answer is no in terms of the structure we set up to begin with. I think that we established and put into effect a superb staff-management system and structure, much of which still survives today, though in very altered forms because you are serving a different president in each administration. The system has to be changed to fit the president.

The thing I wish we had done differently was *not* to have changed the system. It worked superbly well for almost four years. The supreme irony is that a system that did work well and that people who had been familiar with other White Houses felt had worked extremely well, going back to the supreme expert, Bill Hopkins, who'd worked in every White House since Washington, I believe—perhaps it wasn't until Adams.[23] (*Laughter*) Hopkins had started with President Hoover and had been consistently the senior administrative officer in the White House, a career officer, through all those years.

McPherson: Saved us all a lot of grief.

Haldeman: Saved us all a lot of grief, absolutely. He was a marvelous asset to the office.

---

23. Bill Hopkins served every president from 1931 to 1971 as a senior administrative officer in the White House. Throughout the Eisenhower administration his position was executive clerk.

The thing that I wish we had done was to have kept the system intact through the greatest crisis that did hit us, which turned out not to be a foreign crisis of any kind, although it had enormous foreign implications once it did hit. The thing that went wrong is that the system was not followed in the Watergate process from its early rumbling days on through to its acceleration from a "third-rate burglary" to the impeachment of a president.

Had we followed our system, had we dealt with that matter in the way we set up from the outset to deal with all matters, large and small, within a few weeks we would have resolved that matter satisfactorily overall, probably unfortunately for some people, but that was necessary and should have been done. It wasn't done and that led to the ultimate crisis. The fault is not that we had a bad system at all, in my opinion. It's that we didn't use the system when we needed it the most.

Chancellor: General Goodpaster, going back to the Eisenhower years, if you had to do it again, any thoughts?

Goodpaster: As to organization, I think it was very good for those times, for the situation that existed then. Technology was not as far advanced as it is now. We didn't have some of the pressures on the office that exist now, and we had a president who was, if I may say so, the most skillful man when it came to organizing, to performing functions well, with the deepest understanding of the role of organization, of how to use staff, of subordination and decentralization, and so on, of anyone I've ever known or known of.

Chancellor: Was it his wartime experience that did that for him?

Goodpaster: No. The wartime experience was part of it and, of course, his role as commander was a very large part of it. His close association and observation of the British system during his time there also entered into it. But his own experience had gone back a long, long way. When he left Fort Leavenworth and came to Washington, he served as assistant to the assistant secretary of war in the field of logistics. He later was assistant to Douglas MacArthur when MacArthur was chief of staff, and one of the interesting sidelights was that he wrote speeches for MacArthur, which is no small [thing]—and survived. So he had an accumulation of experience. I think that he got a lot out of the American Assembly, a short time at Columbia University, and he brought all of that to bear.[24]

I think that within the organization, the operation was a very effective one.

I was interested in the point about the chief of staff. Governor Sherman Adams, of course, was the chief of staff and later, General Persons. I was staff secretary. But anytime we had a tough personnel decision, I can tell you that Governor Adams was equal to that. A lot of courage and readiness to step up against any difficult problem of that kind. Now, he paid the price for it.

---

24. The American Assembly is a public affairs forum associated with Columbia University.

Chancellor: He was forced to resign.[25]

Goodpaster: On a different issue. But that's not how to win popularity contests around town, to be known as the man who has to exercise that function, but he was ready to step up to it whenever it needed to be done.

If you ask what would you want to do differently, I think that President Eisenhower himself would say that there were some policy areas where he left dissatisfied that he had not accomplished everything that he wished he had accomplished, such as working with the newly independent countries of the world. That was one of his major interests and thrusts, and he simply was not able to accomplish as much there as he hoped to accomplish. Finally, if you ask about specific things, I think if it were May 1, 1960, again, we would not fly the U-2 on that mission.[26]

---

25. For his efficient performance of unpleasant tasks for the Eisenhower White House, Adams earned the epithet "abominable noman." In June 1958 the House Legislative Oversight Committee learned that industrialist Bernard Goldfine had given Adams several gifts, including an oriental rug and a $300 vicuña coat. Apparently, Adams in return intervened with the Securities and Exchange Commission and the Federal Trade Commission to quell probes of Goldfine's business interests. Looking toward the November congressional elections, Republican party regulars pressed for Adams's rapid departure. On September 22, 1958, Eisenhower reluctantly accepted Adams's resignation.

26. On May 1, 1960, a high-altitude U.S. photographic reconnaissance plane was shot down near the Soviet city of Sverdlovsk. The pilot, Francis Gary Powers, was taken prisoner. The incident disrupted the planned Paris summit conference between Eisenhower and Khrushchev. Powers was released in a spy exchange in February 1962.

Chancellor: Yes. I think we can just slide past that, General. (*Laughter*)

Mr. Watson, President Carter organized the White House around his own very good brain, his own dedication to homework and detail. Looking back on that now—and I ask this not in a critical sense—would that be a factor if you were changing how the White House worked under the Carter administration?

Watson: It would, but one thing that you cannot get away from is that the way the White House is organized and the way that it functions are both very much reflections of the man. You take your president as you find him. So to some extent, my sitting here and saying how I would redesign the Carter White House more or less in my own image misses the point. A White House staff has as its function the duty to serve the president in the way that he wishes to be served, to sort of play to his long suits.

Having said that, let me also express a very personal opinion. When we went in, I had a fear and said so to the president in a private memorandum. I said to him that I thought he was one of the brightest, most well-read, most well-educated persons to assume the presidency in the history of the republic; that he was a student of government. He was a voracious reader, a man who wished to know the pros and the cons and the ins and the outs of every issue before him. I said to him, "That's a danger. There's a danger of your overinvolvement. There's a danger of pulling too many things into the White House, and you'll be held accountable for things that you ought not to be held accountable for." As a general observation about our administration, I think we made that mistake. I think the president was involved to too great an extent in too many things. I think we put too many things on the agenda.

In 1977, when he came in, there were simply too many initiatives of too high a level of controversy and complexity that he wanted to do all at once. "Let's pass a national urban policy. Let's pass a comprehensive national energy policy. Let's reorganize the executive branch of government," and so on. "Let's do away with the major boondoggle projects in the West involving water projects and dams and such." Those were things involving huge political capital expenditures, and we did too many things at once.

In terms of organization, if I had to change one thing—and this seems to be a problem that almost every president, though not President Eisenhower, suffers from. They go in with an idea that they are going to have a spokes-of-the-wheel staff. There's going to be equal access.

Chancellor: The president is the hub.

Watson: The president is the hub, and he's going to have *x* number of advisors, six or eight or ten. And because they are all important to him and his friends and counselors and people whose judgment and loyalty he trusts and values, he wants all of them reporting directly to him. He's the hub. That is a fatal mistake. The White House can't operate that way. It pulls the president into too much; he's involved in too many things.

It also results in a lack of cohesion, a lack of organization and cutting in on decision making before it reaches the Oval Office, the presidential level. That was, in my judgment, a mistake that President Carter made in the first two years of his administration. He didn't actually appoint a chief of staff until late in the summer of 1979. I think that many of our problems on the Hill, many of our congressional relationships, difficulties, who's speaking for the president, would have been solved had we started from the very beginning with a strong chief of staff.

McPherson: Really? You mean you would have had a Don Regan in the Carter White House?[27] That kind of an operation?

Watson: No. It's a fair question, Harry, and I'm not necessarily saying that. We were reacting—with all due respect to my good friend, Bob Haldeman—we were reacting to at least a public perception that there had been a kind of palace guard, to quote a colleague of yours, and that there hadn't been a free flow of diverse ideas and information to the president, that it had been too rigidly controlled, too tight a ship. So part of what we were doing was a reaction against

---

27. Donald Regan moved from his post as secretary of the treasury to chief of staff at the White House when he and James Baker swapped jobs at the beginning of President Reagan's second term. As chief of staff, Regan has openly sought to be the central figure of the president's advisory system, describing his role as that of "chief executive officer of the White House." Bernard Weinraub, "How Donald Regan Runs the White House," *New York Times Magazine*, January 5, 1986.

that. As is true of so many things, our pendulum swung too far in the other direction.

The way a White House chief of staff performs his or her function is in itself going to depend on the individual. I think that the way that Jim Baker, to use recent history, performed his role as White House chief of staff for Mr. Reagan, under an organization which was exactly as I'm describing, was very different than the way that Don Regan performs the same role with the same structure. You cannot eliminate or ignore the personal touch of how a particular individual performs a particular job.

But, Harry, my answer to your question is yes, I am suggesting a strong, trusted, even-handed White House chief of staff.

Chancellor: Don Rumsfeld, let me ask you about what Jack Watson has just said about Carter. You worked with Gerald Ford. He was easy to get along with and had more pals tucked here and there in the White House and on the staff. How do you handle a big, genial guy like that, who's always drifting off to have coffee with a buddy in some other office? Wasn't that a problem?

Rumsfeld: There's no question it was a problem. President Ford's whole background was as a legislator. As House minority leader, you have all these spokes coming in to you; you have to deal with them personally. It is a very personal business being minority leader of the United States House of Representatives.

He came into the White House as the first man who had not been elected either as president or vice-president. There was a certain momentum left over from his legislative days, and he fancied that the "spokes of the wheel" was the right way to do it. Al Haig argued against it, Don Rumsfeld argued against it, Dick Cheney argued against it, but the president had to go through his period where he got that out of his system.

In that system, with the spokes coming in, the president is in the center, and the chief of staff is the grease. All the grease does is get overheated and have to be replaced. (*Laughter and applause*)

I'll give you an example of what Jack's talking about. Good motivations, honorable, decent, fine people. Secretary of Labor John Dunlop comes in to see the president; wants to see him alone. Sees him alone. President when he was minority leader always met with legislators alone. What's the problem? Fine. Met with him alone, and they came to some understanding as to what John Dunlop would negotiate with respect to situs picketing, as I recall.[28] And Dunlop went out of the office and proceeded, as an intelligent, honorable, talented man, to do exactly what

---

28. Organized labor had sought passage of federal legislation that would allow a union with a grievance against one contractor to picket all the contractors at the same construction site. (Such picketing, referred to as "common situs picketing," had been ruled illegal by the Supreme Court, citing the ban on secondary boycotts under the Taft-Hartley Act.) Secure with the impression that he had the president's backing, Dunlop testified in behalf of the proposal at congressional hearings. When this position came under attack from Republican constituencies, President Ford reversed course and vetoed the measure. Thomas E. Cronin, *The State of the Presidency*, 2d ed. (Boston: Little, Brown, 1980), p. 259.

he believed the president wanted. The president didn't tell me, didn't tell Dick, didn't tell anybody else what was going on.

Chancellor: Not even "Oh, by the way"?

Rumsfeld: No. And pretty soon, John Dunlop comes back in and reports, "I've done it." And the president looks at it, says, "My gosh, I can't do that, John, and I'm very sorry." Obviously it wasn't what he had intended. Events had intervened and there was no way he could agree to what John had done, and John said, "Well, I can appreciate that, but if you don't do it, I can't stay. My credibility is gone." So you lose a secretary of labor unnecessarily. Two people who were good people, intelligent people, liked each other. Ford didn't want Dunlop to leave. Dunlop didn't want to leave, but there was no way he could stay because of this spokes-of-the-wheel nonsense. There was no question.

Conceivably in Eisenhower's era, conceivably in Kennedy's era, the nature of the world and the size of the White House staff and the nature of the problems, you could have a different arrangement. Today, I do think you need a chief of staff at the White House who has a set of responsibilities that are understood. He has to bring integrity to that staff system. He has to assure that people do get the opportunity to have their voices heard, but he has to be the one who helps the president maintain a certain discipline and order in the process or else the process loses its integrity.

Chancellor: Let me ask Ted Sorensen this because as I recall your stewardship at the White House, your service there, there really wasn't a chief of staff when you came in. Yet you became a kind of chief of staff. Isn't that the way it worked?

Sorensen: Yes and no. During the transition period, I went in to see General Persons, who was the chief of staff, to find out what the drill was. He said, "Not a piece of paper goes into President Eisenhower's desk unless I have initialed it, and other than the press secretary and the secretary of state, no one goes in unless they have come through me first."

John F. Kennedy would not have accepted that system. He would not have been comfortable with me or anyone else operating in that way. So we had a modified system under which one person on policy and program, one person on national security operations, one person on press, and one person on congressional relations each had equal access to the president. We kept in touch with each other, and I think it worked reasonably well without a chief of staff.

Goodpaster: Let me just make a point here. Somewhere between you and General Persons, there was a misunderstanding, because that is not the way it worked and I'm sure that he wouldn't have attempted to convey that. The special assistant for national security affairs had direct access to the president. I, of course, had direct access. The cabinet secretary had direct access. Now, we kept General Persons informed of what we were doing. In my second hat as staff assistant for international operations, I also had direct access to the president. The special counsel, Jerry Morgan, took in every bill, every executive order, every proclamation—either he or Bill Hopkins would take those in. So it was not as controlled, as rigid as you suggest.

Sorensen: No, I didn't mean to say that no one else saw the president. What he indicated to me was that except for the two that he mentioned, everyone else saw the president with his blessing, so to speak, with his imprimatur.

To answer the question about what I would personally have done differently, I would mention two things.

First, on a minor note, I would never have gone back to my home state of Nebraska and delivered a controversial speech which was an invitation to the Republican opposition to jump on me and the president. Indeed, the Republican national committee woman said, "If Ted Sorensen comes back to Nebraska to die, it will be too soon."[29] (*Laughter*)

On a more serious note, I give you a sterling bureaucratic reply: I would have asked for more staff. I'm a great believer in a small staff, but we were stretched way too thin. I had two assistants and we handled all policy, program, messages, speeches, and a lot of politics in addition to that. I did not have time to enjoy what I was doing, to think in terms of the future, and I didn't have enough time to be as nice as I should have been to a lot of people, including congressmen.

---

29. In a July 1961 speech on educational reform, Sorensen ranked Nebraska "among the educationally depressed areas of the country" and called his home state "a good place to come from and a good place to die."

Chancellor: So we have gone in this discussion from the necessity for toughness to the necessity for being nice. I guess both go into the role of a chief of staff.

Watching the evening news

Chancellor: Let's talk about what now seems to be the White House's enormous attention with what's said on the evening news, what's said in the newspapers, and the sort of daily story of what the president is up to that particular day. I think this has changed enormously since the Eisenhower years.

Harry, why don't we start with you?

McPherson: Johnson lived two days in one, literally. He got up in the morning quite early and watched the three television sets in his bedroom, with one of those remote control things. He read all the papers, called people on the Hill, called staff, met with Bill Moyers, Jack Valenti, people like that.[30]

---

30. Bill Moyers directed Johnson's vice-presidential campaign in 1960. In 1963 Moyers was named deputy director of the Peace Corps; in October 1964 Johnson named him special assistant, and from July 1965 until December 1966, when he left Washington, Moyers also served as press secretary. Jack Valenti was director of advertising for Johnson's vice-presidential campaign and became a White House special assistant and speechwriter after Johnson assumed the presidency. Valenti resigned in May 1966 to become president of the Motion Picture Association of America.

Watson: Then he'd have breakfast. (*Laughter*)

McPherson: Then he'd have breakfast. Then he'd work for awhile, come back and have lunch with the last person he met with, and then take a brief nap. He'd had a heart attack, so he was taking care of himself. Sometime about 3:00 or 3:30, frequently he would call me. I guess he called a lot of people, but I could usually count on it in the late afternoon, as he woke up from his nap, that I would get a call which would usually say, "What do you know?"

"Well, what do *you* know?"

"I'm dealing with some minute little question you don't care to know about." But maybe I'd been lucky and had lunch with Evans and Novak.[31] He would want to know what they had said, or more importantly, what I had leaked to them. (*Laughter*)

Then he would start reading the afternoon papers, and then he would want to, of course, see the evening news. There certainly was in him an almost fanatic attention, an interest in everything that was going on—not only about how the Johnson administration was being regarded, but about what was happening.

This whole "spokes-of-the-wheel" business, the whole approach to the president's business, is about information. Our president, unlike the general secretary of the Soviet Union or, well, I guess, a lot of other leaders in the world, does not have an intelli-

---

31. Rowland Evans and Robert Novak are syndicated columnists known principally for their investigative reporting of Washington politics.

gence network throughout the country. He doesn't have, whatever you might think, the FBI doing that.

How does he find out what's going on in the country? How does he get a sense of what's important and how does he get a sense of whom to listen to, where the weight is in the cities and in the agricultural areas?

Chancellor: But he used you as an agent.

McPherson: That's why he has a staff around him of people who have big ears and listen and meet with people all the time and will send him memoranda and will talk to him on the phone and tell him what they think is going on.

Johnson, in the evening, the end of his second day in one, would have a navy guy come in and give him a rubdown and then he'd start reading about 150 memoranda. At the bottom, he would write either yes, no, "see me," or something or other.

Well, every now and then, this would get to be too much for him. So he decided to have a chief of staff, and he picked Bob Kintner, who had been the NBC chairman and had lost his job. He was an old friend of Johnson's, and Johnson thought the world of him. Bob didn't really have a function around the White House for a while. It just coincided that Johnson got tired of reading all these memoranda, and Kintner said, "Why don't I be chief of staff?" So Johnson said fine. He was formerly a network chief of staff. "We will make you the boss."

Well, none of us believed it. We just sent stuff to Johnson as always. Kintner got mad and asked that they all be sent to him. Johnson said, "Well, okay. Send them through Kintner first." We did that.

Lasted about two days. Kintner stopped something. I don't know what it was, some minor piece of business. Johnson got furious and that was the end of Kintner. (*Laughter*)

Ted Sorensen is quite right, and Don is quite right talking about the nature of the fellow, the kind of man he is. It would have been inconceivable to imagine Lyndon Johnson as a Harvard Business School CEO [chief executive officer] coming in—Imagine Lyndon Johnson with a computer, with his PC? (*Laughter*) Inconceivable. On the other hand, he had something that many presidents, many CEOs don't have. Outside of being the smartest man I've ever known, he had twenty-five or thirty years of profound and far-reaching political connections in Washington, which even the smartest president, maybe in just sheer IQ points, Jimmy Carter, did not have.

In 1977 Carter developed that great energy program and tried to put it into effect. When Carter explained it, a Republican congressman whom I respected a lot came back from a meeting up there and said, "That fellow really knows everything about this energy program. Taxes, all of it. He didn't have to call on the secretary of the treasury or energy or any of them. He could do it all." I was bowled over and I said, "Is he going to get it through?" And he said, "I don't know. You know, he's got no agents up here." Having agents throughout the system who want to help you out becomes a very essential part and a nonorganizational part of a successful presidency.

Chancellor: We have talked about the impact of technology, of how fast-flowing information enters into the president's decision-making. It seems to me there's also a great deal of attention being paid now not only to what's coming in, but what the administration is putting out, the daily theme meetings that we saw in the Reagan campaign, for example.

Congressman Cheney, do you suppose that this obsession, it seems to me sometimes, with what the image is on the tube and in print is changing the way decisions are taken in the White House? Let's see if we can take President Reagan out of this; I'm not trying to set this up as an attack on the Reagan administration.

Cheney: I think the Reagan administration is a good one to talk about. Because of President Reagan's personal style, he is especially effective as sort of a symbolic leader of the country. He's very good at using the symbolic aspects of the presidency to talk about themes and concepts, to make people feel good about themselves and about the country. That requires a certain kind of management. But that is the Reagan message, and there's nothing wrong with it.

It may not be as substantive in terms of the nitty-gritty of a budget or tax policy, as Jimmy Carter or Jerry Ford might produce, but it's an integral part of his presidency. I would think if they didn't do it, that he would have been far less effective than he's been in terms of being able to convey that mood and create that feeling that the American people have about him and about the country.

Chancellor: Would you agree with that, Mr. Haldeman? You are a former advertising man. You know a lot about communication.

Haldeman: To a degree, I would, and to a degree, I wouldn't. I think that your point about the obsession in the White House with the image of what goes out is a two-way obsession. I think there's an obsession from outside, the press corps that covers the White House, with every aspect of what's happening in the White House that causes the White House to have to react to those demands, let's say, and to deal with them in a way that then appears as if the White House is obsessed with getting all this out.

I think that the White House press corps, as it's presently constituted, is probably about ten times, and maybe fifty times, too big. I think there are ten times or fifty times too many people accredited to the White House. I think that it's an unwieldy apparatus that is not serving the press, the public, the presidency, or the democracy as the press should be serving it, because there is this obsession with detail and with immediacy.

It gets back to technology again. Everything's got to happen instantly, and a president or his press secretary or any other spokesman who goes out to the briefing room has to respond to the question. If he doesn't respond, it's interpreted as evasion or lying or whatever, when maybe it just isn't time to respond yet. You kind of wish back to the good old days when the reporters submitted their questions a week in advance in writing and the president gave them their answers when he got ready to. I am not suggesting that.

Chancellor: You know what presidents were saying then when reporters were submitting the written questions? They were saying "Can't we get back to the good old days when there were no reporters at all?" (*Laughter and applause*)

Haldeman: There never were those days. And you do want reporters. You do want news reported and the public should know what's happening. The White House, the president and his staff and the rest of the administration, has to be concerned with what is being said on the evening news and in the morning press on a daily, an hourly basis, because the ability to govern depends to a substantial degree in this country upon what the populace thinks you are doing. And what the populace thinks you are doing, they find out from you guys.

President Nixon, as you know, took a decided tactic that was quite effective. Even though he certainly was not regarded as a great communicator in the sense that President Reagan is, he did take the option of going directly to the people fairly frequently with direct television presentations in prime evening time on all three networks. He did it until you guys caught up with the tactic, and the networks started cutting us off so we got on only one at a time. Nobody tuned in then; they all watched the soap opera of the evening.[32]

---

32. During his first nineteen months in office, President Nixon logged over seven hours of appearances on prime time television, much of it in the form of direct addresses to the country. In doing so, Nixon more than doubled Johnson's prime time exposure, and tripled Kennedy's, during comparable periods of their terms. This prompted Dr. Frank Stanton, the president of the Columbia Broadcasting System (CBS), to complain publicly in 1970 that the

But when we had all three networks, there was an opportunity for the president to communicate directly to the American people without being filtered in any way. That did give him an opportunity to make the presentation on major issues that he felt needed to be made. I think that was valuable. I would hope that maybe we could go back to the opportunity for a president to communicate on all three networks, which is almost force-feeding the American populace from time to time by direct communication.

We also need the press corps. We need it somewhat more disciplined than it is today, and disciplined by itself probably, not by the White House. I think we need it reduced, but I think the getting out of information is vitally important, and we have to learn to deal with the new technology and the new situation. It's somewhat, though, a bum rap to put an obsession with image solely on the White House. I think it is a two-way obsession. I think the media are obsessed with the White House as much as the White House is obsessed with the media.

White House was trying to monopolize the airwaves. Voicing the same complaint, the Democratic National Committee began asking the networks for response time to the president's addresses; by and large, their requests were granted. The Federal Communications Commission took the unprecedented action of invoking the "fairness doctrine" during a nonelection period and granting critics of the administration's Vietnam policies airtime to state their views. On these events and their long-term effects on network policies, see Samuel Kernell, *Going Public: New Strategies of Presidential Leadership* (Washington, D.C.: CQ Press, 1986) pp. 91 and 102–3.

Rumsfeld: A step further. Why in the world are these eight or ten grown men sitting here in a semicircle? (*Laughter*)

Haldeman: Because of that camera over there.

Rumsfeld: Exactly. It's because some very smart person decided that this was an effective way to communicate on this subject, and that's why we are doing this, in this most unnatural kind of a setting. That's what the president does. He says, "I need to communicate. How do I go about doing it? What's the most effective way of reaching the people?"

Chancellor: Yes, but what bothers me is that I find that instead of just being there open for questioning, the way it seems to work in the White House is that you all have gotten together, had a serious meeting, and agreed on four simply understood Wheaties-box statements that you could make. Then you come out, and that's all the country gets.

Haldeman: I have to interject. If we didn't do that, you or your producer would do it, [Tom] Brokaw or his producer would do it, and they would come on and select the four little gems that were to be condensed, because you have thirty million hours of news that you condense into less than thirty minutes and zap it out to the folks. Our option is: Do we decide that *you* should decide what are the key points, or do we decide what are the key points?

Chancellor: That is very validly put.

Haldeman: And I think it should be us, not you.

Haig: The question is, Has modern technology, television, changed the style of every White House? The answer is, of course it has. But there is an underlying question here, Do presidents conduct their affairs by getting up each morning and putting their finger to the wind to see what was said on the tube the night before and then develop policies to be responsive to that?

There is a growing trend to do that. I happen to think that it's both bad politics and bad policy. And I think the American people are too smart, over the long run, to support that kind of "populism." The people are interested essentially in results, not in the pandering day to day to their whims.

Chancellor: I'm hearing a theme, General, that's fascinating. It's a kind of a Luddite idea: If you could cut back the pace of technology, if you could separate the president a little bit from all of this, incoming and outgoing, you might be better off.

The media: Box-tops and bumper stickers

Chancellor: Let me ask several of you a question. When you were a senior official in the White House, did you appear regularly on television? You can answer just yes or no. I'm trying to prove a point.

Goodpaster: Certainly not. We really had only two spokesmen in the White House. One was the press secretary, Jim Haggerty, and the other was none other than Dwight D. Eisenhower.

Chancellor: Mr. Sorensen, did you, when you were a senior official, appear regularly on television?

Sorensen: No. To the best of my recollection, during those years, I appeared only once. It was on "Meet the Press" and my chief responsibility was to say nothing. The show had barely ended when a phone rang right in the studio. They said, "It's for you," and a familiar voice said, "They didn't lay a glove on you." (*Laughter*)

Chancellor: Mr. Haldeman, when you were a senior official of the White House, did you appear regularly on television or in print?

Haldeman: I never appeared by my own act or initiative, never on television or in print. Our staff approached the structure of the White House staff very seriously, adhering to Brownlow's theory of the passion for anonymity and the point that a staff person to the president could maintain his value only if he said what he had to say to the president and the staff, but *not* to the world.[33] The operative people, department

---

33. In 1936 President Roosevelt appointed Louis Brownlow to chair a committee on administrative management in the executive branch. The recommendations of that committee have become the blueprint for the modern institutional presidency, and they are referred to several times by the panelists in these discussions. "The president needs help," the committee stated bluntly at the beginning of its report, which then outlined two structures for presidential assistance: the Executive Office of the President, which was to include the Bureau of the Budget (then housed in the Treasury Department) and a new White House office. The latter was to

heads, and the president himself were the people who would speak to the world about what the administration was doing. That was our intent going in.

It was the position that I took consistently until I was urged by the press to go on that one interview show that I did. I made the statement that I was told to make, and the press staff instantly concluded that was enough of me on television, thank goodness, and I didn't go on anymore.

Chancellor: When you were working for Ford, Congressman Cheney, it began to change a little bit then, didn't it? Didn't I see you on television more than I had seen your predecessor?

Cheney: Only once. I did exactly the same thing Ted did only on another network, "Face the Nation." It was really a put-up deal with some of my friends in the press corps. I talked to the press frequently but always on background, always to explain policy, never to be quoted, never to be out front as a public official.

Bob is absolutely right, that was the philosophy we tried to pursue. I think the big shift has really been with the Reagan administration.

Chancellor: I think so.

Cheney: I think it's occurred in part because it's been the way they have decided to operate, but also because

---

be staffed by six personal assistants, whose service to the president required them, the committee intoned, to have "a passion for anonymity." On the development of the modern institutional presidency, see Peri E. Arnold, *Making the Managerial Presidency* (Princeton, N.J.: Princeton University Press, 1986).

the president delegates so much authority. There's perhaps even more intense focus now from the press on the senior staff than there's ever been before.

Rumsfeld: My experience was the same. As chief of staff, I don't believe I was on television but once or twice, and it was at the insistence of the president, feeling I should go on for some particular reason.

Haldeman: As soon as you do that, you become the issue. As soon as you become the issue, you've lost an enormous amount of your value to the president, in my opinion, as a staff person.

Chancellor: Well, Mr. Watson, in the Carter administration, we saw a lot of the national security advisor, Zbigniew Brzezinski, on television, didn't we?

Watson: Too much. (*Laughter*)

Haldeman: Well, you did see Henry Kissinger occasionally during our time.

Chancellor: We did, but he went through an interesting transformation from the unquotable German-accented official to somebody who was all over the place.

Haldeman: That's right.

Chancellor: When I was growing up, it was said that anybody who gets to be president will grow in the office: The office makes the man. Do any of you have any thoughts on that?

Cheney: Yes, I would say it has an enormous impact. Even a man like Jerry Ford, who was near the end of a long, distinguished political career and had firm practices and values in mind when he arrived—it changed him in fairly fundamental ways, especially in terms of his style of operation. He became a much tougher critic in the quality of his staff work, a much better judge of people, tougher on himself in terms of what he thought was acceptable. He also became much more confident of his own judgments. He watched bright and able and talented people work for him and sometimes make mistakes, and I think he quickly developed a recognition that his judgment was as good or better than theirs.

Watson: May I make a brief point? I think a president can work too hard at the job. I think Carter worked too hard. I think that one needs to find a balance— meaning no disrespect at all—find a balance between Mr. Reagan's schedule and short day and the other extreme of having the president involved in too much detail and to too great an extent. I think the president can overexpose himself.

I think one of the things that President Reagan does perhaps as well as any person who's ever been in that office is measure out his exposure. I know that that's not something that the press likes, but I think the president has to limit his exposure. Someone said one time to me, and to others, I'm sure, in this semi- circle, "Don't try to communicate anything to the American people over television that's too compli- cated to be put on a bumper sticker." (*Laughter*)

Chancellor: That's very good. I learned that a long time ago.

Sorensen: There's no question that the world looks very different from inside the White House than from outside. You can be a good senator or congressman or politician if you make a strong speech or if you raise the right question or if you sound the alarm. None of that does you any good at all when you are in the White House and you are responsible for running the show. You have to come up with the answers. Being in the Oval Office exerts a tremendous impact on the individual.

Chancellor: Growth?

Sorensen: He may grow, which I happen to think Kennedy and others did, but it may also break you. I would not want the American people to think we can elect a mediocrity to the White House because he will grow.

Goodpaster: I think I've seen in every president, and I know that I saw it in President Eisenhower, a concern for the protection of the institution of the presidency. I have just one little memory of that.

One day, President Eisenhower had Senator Lyndon Johnson in the office for a private meeting of the kind that he often had with him and with Sam Rayburn. As they were leaving, Eisenhower was concerned about something that might happen in the Congress. It might have been the Bricker amendment;[34] it was something like that, that could dimin-

---

34. In January 1953 Senator John W. Bricker (R–Ohio) proposed an amendment to the Constitution that would have defined "the legal aspect of certain treaties and executive agreements." The measure was widely recognized as an effort to curb a president's treaty-making power. At the time of this conversation, Lyndon Johnson was majority leader in the Senate, and Sam Rayburn was Speaker of the House.

ish the authority, the power of the president. And President Eisenhower said, "Lyndon, be careful what you do because someday, you may be sitting in this chair." Now, that was a thought that Lyndon Johnson received with great pleasure, I can tell you. (*Laughter*)

It was partly tactical, I think, on Eisenhower's part, but it was also substantive. Lyndon Johnson was then the majority leader of the Senate, and the president wanted to share with him a sense of the importance of maintaining the institution of the presidency so that it could serve our country effectively in the future. I later recalled that day to President Johnson, and he remembered it just as clearly as I did. It was a day that stayed in his memory.

Hit the ground running

Chancellor: Mr. Haldeman, it's been said that if you don't know what you want to do when you get into the White House, you'll never find out once you are there. Did you all have a plan? I mean, what Jack Watson was talking about, the great dreams and hopes and programs of the Carter administration. Did the Nixon administration in 1969 have an overall plan?

Haldeman: Very much so.

Chancellor: And you think that's a good idea?

Haldeman: Absolutely. I think it's essential that a president, first of all, have a vision which precedes the plan of what he's trying to accomplish. Obviously, in office he's restricted by circumstances.

President Nixon was restricted in time and opportunity because of the Vietnam War. He fully expected, totally expected in his own mind that the Vietnam War would be negotiated to a settlement by the fall of 1969, within the first six to eight months of his administration, and that from then on, he could move forward with his agenda for building a structure of world peace. That was his overriding vision, not just a peaceful situation, but a structure, an institution that would maintain world peace in the future. He also envisioned some substantial work in revising the domestic structure and the office of the presidency, the Executive Office of the President and the executive branch of the government. He wanted to leave in place a domestic structure and an international structure that would be a framework for the future.

The specifics that fleshed out that vision were worked up by then-candidate Nixon and a number of academic and practical task-force people in a number of areas. Arthur Burns directed that activity, and Paul McCracken.[35] There is a fascinating set of papers that covers what was the Nixon agenda. It's also fascinating how much of that agenda, despite the delay

---

35. Arthur W. Burns served as counselor to the president in the first Nixon administration and then became chairman of the Federal Reserve Board. Paul McCracken served Nixon as chairman of the Council of Economic Advisors.

through the entire first term of ending the Vietnam War, was either implemented or at least started. The tragedy was that at the end the president's power to govern and to initiate became totally diffused by his necessity, as Al pointed out, just to survive.

If there had been a full second term and if the agenda could have been carried out, I think you would have seen a grand plan well underway, if not totally executed. Because there wasn't, much of that plan fell by the wayside in midstream.

Chancellor: About a third of our presidents, Harry, have come into the office, say, on the death of a president, without that kind of preparation. Lyndon Johnson came in that way, with no grand plan. Can you contrast his attitude to what Bob Haldeman has told us about Nixon?

McPherson: When you talk about a grand plan, having one or not having one, it sounds as if the man is operating in a vacuum. But in fact, all the people we are talking about, presidents of the United States, became president, in part, in reaction to something that had happened before, even in Lyndon Johnson's case.

A southerner, a politician, a very good politician, who had represented a southern state and then the Democratic party in the Senate, was suddenly thrown into the presidency. All sorts of things played upon his Great Society program as he developed it. In his first speech, he said, "Let us continue." He wanted to show the country that a parvenu had not come in, a usurper, or—in very specific terms—a conspirator from Texas, where President Kennedy had been assassinated, had not come in to replace and disrupt and throw away the movement of the New Frontier and its programs.

He also meant to show that he was a national politician, that he cared, that he wasn't just a white politician, that he was going to do something in the field of civil rights, and for old people and their medical care, and for education. He was going to use his time in office and use it quickly and urgently to get a lot done.

By the end of the first year of his full term, 1965, he had passed everything except Mother's Day resolutions. Congress had worked late every night; they were exhausted. On the urging of the *Washington Post*, he tried to get Congress to pass home rule for the District of Columbia, the last thing that was on the shelf.[36] He failed. We failed. And the *Washington Post*, astonishingly, criticized him for trying to do too much at the end.

I thought he would be furious at that, but he said, "No, that's right, I did try to do too much. But you know, you've only got one year. No matter what your mandate is and vote, you've only got a year because in the second year, you will have done a lot of things that will make even people in your own party want to put distance between themselves and you." And poignantly, this was the end of 1965, he said, "If this war goes on another year, there will be a lot of those."

---

36. The legislation provided for election of a mayor, a partisan legislative council, a nonpartisan board of education, and a nonvoting delegate to the House of Representatives. Every president since Truman had submitted similar legislation. In 1973 home rule for the District of Columbia was finally approved.

And then in the third year, you've lost a lot of your votes usually, the mid term, you lose a lot of your strength in the Congress. The fourth year is all presidential politics. So in Johnson's mind, anyway, you had one year. President Reagan hit the ground running in 1981 with his budget cuts and his tax program, trying to effectuate his policy.

But it's not as if fellows sit in universities or in law offices or in other places abstracted from a real world. They come in, they get on this escalator at high speed, and they do their best, under the limitations of their humanity, to cope with it and to try to induce it to behave somewhat better for themselves and the country.

Chancellor: On that note, gentlemen, I want to thank you all for being with us, sitting here in the tribal circle. You are people who obviously served your presidents very well and your country very well.

The one thing that I'd bring out of having known you over the years, many of you, and talked to you here today, is the degree of care and concern not only for the president, but for the country and the institution of the presidency. It's been an honor for me to have been with you, and I thank you very much.

★ 2 ★

The View from the Inside

This second session of the conference, held on the afternoon of January 17, 1986, was devoted to questions from invited scholars and the general public. In order, the questioners are: Samuel Popkin, department of political science, University of California, San Diego; Bradley Patterson, Brookings Institution; Larry Berman, department of political science, University of California, Davis; Quinn Hornday, Bill Otterson, and Frank Gormley, all San Diego residents; Doug Newhart, a university student; Fred Greenstein, department of politics, Princeton University; and Samuel Kernell, Brookings Institution.

Campaigning versus governing

Samuel Popkin: I'd like to draw on two comments that the panelists made this morning and ask them to elaborate, and they both deal with the differences between campaigning and governing. One of the panelists mentioned that the fourth year of a term is all presidential politics. Another panelist mentioned that in the first year, you are not equipped to deal with anything except presidential politics. So at least half of the time you are in the White House, you are either recovering from or preparing for an electoral campaign. I'm curious, from the inner circle chief's perspective, what problems you have had coordinating the ongoing process of holding the government together and the demands of the next primary or of the next deal that must be made as part of the building of electoral coalitions to govern?

Haldeman: I'll take that for a minute, because I'd like to respond in a dissenting note maybe from what was said this morning. I think that that was said in terms of generalities. I don't think that whoever said it meant that you couldn't do anything *but* recover from the campaign in the first year nor that you couldn't do anything *but* get ready for the campaign in the fourth year, but rather that those were areas in which focus inevitably fell in those two years in the presidency. But I don't think there's all that much difference between campaigning and governing in a lot of aspects.

The president in a campaign or the candidate in a campaign develops his platform, develops his concepts of what he's going to do. When he comes into office, he comes in running hard. He's got a honeymoon with Congress in the first year. He's got an opportunity to do a lot of things. True, he doesn't yet have a staff seasoned in governing, seasoned in operating a White House, and it's tough for the staff. I don't think it's all that tough for the president himself in the first year.

In the fourth year, getting ready for the reelection campaign, assuming that the president is running for reelection, is not totally a bad exercise in good government, either, because what you are doing to be reelected may very well be what the electorate wants you to do as president. I don't think the responsiveness that is sharpened by the forthcoming campaign is necessarily a bad thing in government.

McPherson: I'm at a disadvantage in that I never took part in a campaign. I spent a couple of months in early 1968 writing what I thought was a speech in which we would scale down the war and appeal for peace and then get ready to run for reelection. And President Johnson made my speech, and then he added a little epilogue.[1] (*Laughter*) So I don't know.

I'm the one who said, or quoted Johnson as saying, you only have one year. He thought the first year was the one in which you had all the momentum from the

---

1. The surprise epilogue Johnson added was his announcement that he would not run for reelection: "With America's sons in the fields far away, with America's future under challenge right here at home, with our hopes and the world's hopes for peace in the balance every day, I do not believe that I should devote an hour or a day of my time to any personal partisan causes or to any duties other than the awesome duties of this office—the Presidency of your country. Accordingly, I shall not seek, and I will not accept, the nomination of my party for another term as your President."

mandate and went forward, as Reagan did with his budget in '81.

As a footnote, I want to state what I suppose is a divergence of opinion between me and Bob Haldeman.

I think it is better not to staff the White House solely or even largely with people whose only experience of governing is campaign experience. I just don't think that's a good idea. Perhaps that's very much a special pleading, because the Johnson staff was not staffed with campaign people but with people who had spent a good deal of time in government in one place or another. You probably need both. Probably helps the president, since it's a political office, to have campaign people, but I would like to see presidents bring in and have about them people who are familiar with the way the federal government operates and with its limitations as well as its possibilities.

Haldeman: You are not diverging from me at all in that. I totally agree with you.

Cheney: Let me take just a slightly different tack from Bob Haldeman. I really think you could make the case that the last year, the campaign year—maybe it was unique in the Ford administration, I doubt it— has enormous impact on what you can do. It's not so much a matter that you shade your policy or avoid doing things that need to be done. But if you are in the middle of a tough, knock-down, drag-out campaign, it limits your ability to get things done. There's nothing to focus the mind on your priorities—whether it's electioneering, getting reelected, or governing—like a thirteen-hundred–vote victory in the New Hampshire primary. That really brings into very sharp focus exactly what it is you want to do.

During the Ford years, for example, the negotiations with the Soviets and the SALT Treaty became an issue in the campaign itself. In the interest of preserving the SALT option, in the interest of not politicizing the whole arms-control process, the issue sort of went on the back burner, so it didn't get mixed up in the campaign, but it did delay and defer policy.[2]

Chancellor: Any thoughts over here?

Watson: I'll just make one quick point. I think that our primary election process right now is debilitating to the country and to the government. It lasts too long. We really ought not to have primaries that go on for months and months and months. (*Applause*) So that one thing we could do, in response to Sam's question as to the governing in the last year, would be to revise our rules so that we are dealing with the primary election process in a greatly foreshortened period of time.

---

2. Cheney is referring to ratification of SALT II, the second round of the Strategic Arms Limitations Talks treaty, which President Ford and Soviet Premier Leonid Brezhnev negotiated at the Vladivostok summit in November 1974. The agreement limits the numbers of intercontinental ballistic missiles, multiple-warhead nuclear weapons, and the production of long-range bombers. Although SALT II was never ratified by the U.S. Senate, both countries continue to observe the arms-control limits.

The ghost ship of government

Bradley Patterson: My question is a question about the size of the White House staff. Every White House staff group, as you go through history, looks to the one that came after it and shakes its head in dismay and says "My God, that's just too many people." The people in the Truman White House look at what came after them and they say "This is just terrible"; the Eisenhower folks look at what came after them and they say "This is just out of control."

Rumsfeld: They were all right. (*Laughter*)

Patterson: What should be, if any, the limits on White House staff size? Does one get to the point where a chief of staff would say, "Hey, this is too big"?

Rumsfeld: There's a natural tendency for staffs to grow. When I was chief of staff for the White House, we did, in fact, reduce it. In my judgment, presidents have different needs, and to the extent that you can move more things out from the departments, just as in a corporation or any other activity, you are better off.[3] At G. D. Searle, I reduced the staff from 850, when I arrived, to 147. And it worked better.

⋅ It takes someone who decides that it's important that you not bring every problem into the White House but, in fact, push them out.

---

3. President Ford, committed to reducing the size of his staff, eliminated thirty-five positions, or about 8 percent of the staff allocations he inherited from President Nixon.

To give an example. The Press Secretary in the White House is asked a question by a member of the White House press corps about agriculture. He's got a choice: either he answers it or he says that's a question that should be directed to the Department of Agriculture. Now, the person asking the question doesn't want to go to the department because his paper already has someone covering the Agriculture Department. He wants the story, and so he presses and presses. Finally the press secretary caves in, and pretty soon every question in the world is being answered by the White House press secretary, which is goofy, and then you need a giant White House press staff. Whereas basically, a lot of that should be shoved out. That's true of issue after issue. It's true of substantive jurisdiction.

Haig: The simple facts are that this horrendous growth in the White House staff has been paralleled by an even more horrendous growth in the congressional staffs, where today I think you are looking at a figure of about twenty thousand.[4] A White House has to respond to that behemoth, and therefore it's a natural contributor to this growth.

The other gimmick, which Bob Haldeman will re-

---

4. Between the mid-1950s and the early 1980s, the growth of staff in Congress and its committees more than matched that of the White House. The staff of the members' offices increased from 3,556 in 1957 to 11,432 in 1981; the number of committee staffers rose from 715 in 1955 to 2,865 in 1981. Norman J. Ornstein and others, *Vital Statistics on Congress, 1984–1985 Edition* (Washington, D.C.: American Enterprise Institute, 1984), pp. 121 and 124.

member, is that administrations that want to show they are lean and mean merely keep the fellows they have but charge them to the departments. It's nicer anyway, because the department has to pay and those fellows are counted on the department's books and not counted by the White House press who are looking for this growth.

I share Don Rumsfeld's view very, very vigorously. Cutting down the staff—and I know Bob tried to cut it down, I know Don did, I know I did—is the best way. The leaner and meaner you are, the more effective your White House will be.

Watson: Another point, as a matter of clarification. There are about fifteen hundred people in the Office of Management and Budget, which is part of the Executive Office of the President. The White House staff is about 350 or less, generally speaking, and is just one of the components of the executive office.

What runs the numbers of presidential staffers up higher are the Council of Economic Advisors, the Council on Environmental Quality, and other such groups that are in the executive office.

Haig: What's material is who gets in the White House Mess, who gets a parking place. (*Laughter*) If you have been involved in the bureaucratic in-fighting, try to decide that.

Watson: I'll make a suggestion, as a general proposition—and we were victims of this, so I'm speaking out of bitter experience here. There began a tendency, I suspect under President Johnson, but we took it to its full flower, of bringing into the White House what's called a special assistant to the president for Hispanic affairs, for women's affairs, for consumer affairs, for elderly affairs, for minority affairs. Please, don't misunderstand my point. I'm not saying that the president and the policies that the president endorses and promotes from the White House ought not to be sensitive and responsive to that enormously wide array of interests. Those are legitimate interests.

But I do not think you need to have a special assistant to the president for every legitimate special interest in the country. But for a time there was, though I think it's been cut back now because, in my judgment, it was so clearly the wrong way to go. There was a tendency between 1965, I'd say, and 1980 for that to happen more and more, and that's one of the things that made the White House staff grow.

Sorensen: More important than who gets a White House parking permit or who eats in the White House Mess is who is able to invoke the president's name, who is using the president's telephone, and who is using the president's stationery. That's serious. If you have hundreds of people doing that, there is no way you can keep them out of mischief.

I have hanging on my wall a picture which shows a dozen individuals, roughly a dozen, standing on the back steps of the White House. That was the senior professional staff, the professional staff of the White House at that time. A couple of them, I'm not quite sure what they did, to tell you the truth. To have a similar group picture now, you would need Yankee

Stadium. (*Laughter*) That's because we have people in the White House who are operating and administering programs without ever having been confirmed by the Senate. It's because we have people in the White House, as Jack Watson says, who aren't there representing the president to the country. They are representing the country to the president. That's not what the White House staff should be.

Rumsfeld: I want to add something that I think hits something quite important about the problem of the president. President Kennedy was concerned about poverty. As I recall, he formed the Committee on Juvenile Delinquency. Pretty soon, in the Executive Office of the President under Lyndon Johnson came the Office of Economic Opportunity, which Sargent Shriver ran, and whom I succeeded. Now here you have two or three thousand employees in the Executive Office of the President in an operating agency that doesn't belong there.

The reason President Johnson did it was not because he was stupid or a bad manager. He did it because President Kennedy was assassinated. He did it because the department's agencies weren't doing things the way he wanted, so he decided he had to have it in the White House.

Same thing with President Nixon. He was concerned about the drug problem. What's he do? Special office for drug abuse, and the next thing you know, you have a whole bunch of people to deal with, a whole bunch of employees, and pretty soon, they are operating programs. Now that's, in fact, bad management.

The answer is not to substitute and layer in the White House. The answer is to make the departments and agencies do that which you believe they ought to be doing. It's a lot harder, takes more time, and it takes ultimately some cooperation with the Congress, but in the last analysis, we would just sink if we keep adding special offices in the Executive Office of the President, even for good reason.

Chancellor: Some of us in the press—and I speak for myself—are not so much worried about the *size* of the White House staff, which when I last looked it up was six hundred, and the expense, which was $22 million—I will avoid all comparisons with ashtrays and toilet seats. (*Laughter*) Rather, it's what they do with it, and I think your point is absolutely right. What do these people do? If they did their jobs in a really super way, a decent managerial way, I think that the question about staff size would go away completely. Not that I think there are an awful lot of people in the White House who are just sitting around doing nothing. I think they work pretty hard.

Sorensen: That's what worries me.

Chancellor: That's what worries you. There's too much of it. I think the question about the size of the staff is not irrelevant, but it's what they do with it to support the running of the government that I think is most important.

Larry Berman: Not too long ago I read General Haig's book in which he referred to the anonymous White

House aides, the ghost ship of government.[5] I guess things sometimes look different when you are a secretary of state compared to a member of a White House staff.

When the Brownlow commission gave forth its recommendations, it called for a small White House staff which would be relatively anonymous, one whose power would be in proportion to the restraint in which it exercised its responsibilities. And perhaps most important, the commission foresaw the greatest danger arising if members of the White House staff were to ever shut the president off from those who are constitutionally responsible, the cabinet officers. Over the last thirty years the swelling of the White House staff has been at the cost of cabinet government.

As I understand it, General Haig, when you were secretary of state, the frustration seemed quite different from when you worked in the White House. General Haig, do you think the Brownlow plan has any relationship whatsoever to the realities of 1986?

Haig: Yes, yes, because it takes one to know one. Having come from the White House staff, I was very sensitive to the tendency for the White House staff to assume authority and responsibility which, by the confirmation process, belongs quite rightly in the hands of the cabinet officers and the cabinet departments. I wrote about this in excruciating detail in my book,

---

5. Berman is referring to Alexander Haig's *Caveat: Realism, Reagan, and Foreign Policy* (New York: Macmillan, 1984).

about this tendency for the White House staff to put themselves in a position where they determine policy and act in behalf of the president across the full range of our policy. It is a very, very dangerous, pernicious reality today. I think here, again, however, it depends on the president and what he wishes.

I would hope that our presidents would be more sensitive to the danger of staff people running government. A staff officer should be a catalyst, a communicator. He should facilitate the ability of the cabinet officer to bring his views to the president, and above all, never be a blockage. I've seen it work both ways; most recently, the wrong way, in my view.

Haldeman: I've seen it only from the White House side, and I completely agree with Al, and I completely agree with the Brownlow plan, that the White House staff should be an operational unit, not a policy-making or policy-executing unit. It should be there to assist the president in the management of the executive branch and in the office of the president, and it should exist at and operate at the will and direction of the president. I think it's imperative that that be the case and it's essential, in order to do that, that virtually all the staff members, except perhaps the press secretary and one or two other designated spokesmen, be people with Brownlow's "passion for anonymity."

Goodpaster: I don't think it's all that difficult, because I saw President Eisenhower, in fact, operate along these lines. I remember a very sharp question that he addressed to members of the staff on occasion, or a comment, and it ran like this, "Now, wait a minute, boys. That's not a staff matter. That's a policy matter, and if I'm going to consider that, I want the secretary of state here. I want the cabinet to consider that. I want the NSC [National Security Council] to consider it." That was part of his process of pushing operational decisions to the operating departments and agencies where he thought they belonged. So I think it can be done.

Sorensen: I agree with all of that, but I want to add the important legal footnote. The Constitution does not call for cabinet government. Indeed, it doesn't say anything about a cabinet whatsoever. The executive power is vested in the president of the United States, and because the Founding Fathers had great confidence in George Washington, whom they knew would be the first president, they left it very vague and wide open compared to the very specific details they put in the Constitution regarding Congress. So each president is free to organize the executive branch as he sees fit.

He can have cabinet government and put issues to a vote of the cabinet if he wishes, though I can't imagine any modern president doing that. Or he can take more and more power into the White House, if he wishes. I happen to think, as my colleagues do, that too much power in the White House and not enough reliance on the cabinet officers individually is a grave error. But we should always remember that the Constitution leaves the president free to take the approach that fits him best.

Rumsfeld: I think the phrase "cabinet government" is not a good one because it leaves people with the impression that it's possible today to allow cabinet officers to proceed semi-independently in their respective areas of jurisdiction. The way our world works, it's rare when you find an issue that is the jurisdiction of only one cabinet officer.

Take a grain embargo with Poland for example. Imposing an embargo or terminating one obviously is a foreign policy issue. It may very well be a Defense Department issue. It's clearly a Treasury issue on the balance of payments. It may be a Department of Labor issue because in some cases, the unions have refused to load. It's obviously a congressional issue. It's certainly going to be a press issue. You have all these threads, and the White House staff's function is to see that those threads get through the needle's eye in a reasonably coherent way. The staff's job is not to make the decisions, but by the same token, the staff has to avoid letting the president be blind-sided by allowing a single cabinet officer to go out and make a decision like that, because he can't.

McPherson: Which is why you need a substantial White House staff. That's why it developed. It didn't happen just because some megalomaniac like Lyndon Johnson said, "Let's add them all up." It didn't happen that way at all.

These interdepartmental committees, the Office of Economic Opportunity, which was put in the White House staff for a very long time, didn't happen just because Johnson thought that was a swell idea, getting kind of bored with cabinet government and that sort of thing. It happened because the whole notion of a broad-scale attack on poverty involved education, employment and training of all kinds, juvenile delinquency prevention, and so on. Everybody with a little fiefdom out there, all the [Civil Service] GS-15s and 16s, and maybe the politicians who got appointed to be cabinet officers, wanted to have their own ballgame. And if you wanted all of it to cohere, you had to put somebody above it. You knew you had to have somebody kind of looking over things. That's why there was a director of the Office of Economic Opportunity though he didn't have to necessarily be in the White House, as he turned out to be.

But as to the main function of a White House staffer, I considered it my main function to be trying, as Don says, to help all those strands come through in a coherent way and then to give President Johnson the best judgment I could, which on occasion he accepted, as to whether what he was doing made sense from the national interest and from Lyndon Johnson's interest. The two were not—even I perceived that sometimes they were not the same. If we said to him, "This is something that can do you some political good but it's a bad idea"—everybody up here has said that—we were exercising a function that most frequently will not be exercised by a cabinet officer. They are out there running their own game very much.

You have a cabinet meeting, and I've tried to think, ever since I've observed them, how to hold a good one. Say you've got a grain embargo issue, or let's say you have an issue on the farm bill or an issue on Vietnam or whatever. Let's say it's Vietnam, and you turn

to the secretary of interior and you say, "Stu Udall,
what do you think about it?"[6]

"Well, you know, I've been thinking about the National Park Service, not about Vietnam."

"Dean Rusk, what do you think about the Park Service?" But he hasn't been thinking about parks at all.

So you need some people who are looking at the en-
tirety of government as much as possible from the
president's senior political point of view, from the
point of view of his responsibility. That's why the
staff grew. Probably ought to be smaller, but it can't
be too much smaller without weakening the chief political officer.

Goodpaster: Let me add just one more point on procedure, and I'm sure that every president in every presidency used this procedure.

When an issue such as the one Don Rumsfeld cites
comes up, it is the duty of the staff, first of all, to call
on people to get their facts in hand and prepare themselves, and if it's an important issue, to bring in the
people who have responsibility so that they can sit in
front of the president and the thing can be shredded
out. These are the so-called ad hoc meetings in the
president's office and they address a particular issue.

If there's established policy, the president will consider whether the policy fits the situation, whether
some adjustment needs to be made. Or if there is no
policy, he'll step up to the decision.

---

6. Stewart Udall served as secretary of the interior from 1961
through the end of Johnson's term. Dean Rusk, mentioned next,
was secretary of state under Kennedy and Johnson.

One of the techniques used by Eisenhower, and I'll cite it again, was to require, when that happened, that everybody speak his piece, that there could be no nonconcurrence through silence. If somebody disagreed, he was responsible for speaking up. But once the issue had been considered and a decision made, then the president expected, first, that it would be a recorded decision and, second, that people would go out and carry it into effect within their respective areas.

If some decision required reconsideration, if it broke down in some way, the understanding was, "We will all be back here again and we will face the president again." I can tell you that that tended to encourage successful implementation of his decisions. They did not like to repeat that experience too often.

Chancellor: I think I ought to add something about the historical background. The cabinet system, Ted, to which you referred, really came up out of politics and not out of constitutional law.[7] In an earlier and less media-ridden age, a president would go to the country with the cabinet officers he would propose, and they each had their own independent political base. I always felt, growing up, that that was a wonderful system because their threatening to resign was a

---

7. Four cabinet departments were established by acts of Congress in 1789: Foreign Affairs, Treasury, War, and Attorney General. Interior was added in 1849, Agriculture in 1862, Labor in 1903, and Commerce in 1913. Since the Eisenhower administration, five new departments have been created: Health, Education and Welfare (1953), Housing and Urban Development (1965), Transportation (1966), Energy (1977), and Education (1979).

limit on the power of a runaway president. But listening here today to you and to some of the others, I think we are not talking about a cabinet. We are talking about a dozen GS-18s appointed by the president. I just want to ask everyone for a yes or no answer to a question, Should White House chiefs of staff be confirmed by the Senate?

Cheney: No.

Haig: No.

McPherson: No.

Haldeman: Absolutely not.

Goodpaster: No.

Watson: No.

Rumsfeld: I'm shocked that you asked.

Sorensen: No.

Chancellor: Okay, next question. That's the only time they've agreed all day.

National security: Too many cooks?

Quinn Hornday: I'll address this question to Mr. Haldeman. Is there within the operations of the presidency a program for study and development of peace

through means other than the conventional battle-
ship diplomacy?

Haldeman: That depends on the particular office of the
particular president at any given time. There is, I'm
sure, in the office of every president the effort to work
in that direction, but it's done in different ways by
different presidents with different staff structures.

Chancellor: Anybody else have any thoughts? There have
been proposals over the years that more institutional
attention be paid to peace.

Haldeman: The last thing you need is more institutions.

Chancellor: General Haig, what about it? What if you
were president and I came to you and said I think we
have to have a Department of Peace. We have a Department of Defense, now we need a Department of
Peace.

Haig: I don't want this to sound too outrageous because
there have been a number of legislative proposals to
develop a Peace Department, so to speak. But I think
that if you are conducting your Department of State
properly and your Department of Defense and other
security-related agencies properly, that's precisely
what their charge is. I wouldn't want a vested interest that dealt with a question of peace in isolation because our defense establishment and our diplomacy
are all predicated on the need, in the nuclear age in
particular, to preserve peace, and we want them to be
advocates for it and not have some special group with
an endowed responsibility to fight for peace. Everyone must do that.

Chancellor: I think that's what makes a lot of people uneasy, General. With all respect, I think that's what makes people say, "Gee, you know, they say the Department of Defense and Caspar Weinberger are fighting for peace." (*Laughter*) Okay? (*Applause*) The problem is that Secretary Weinberger and the department haven't given the public that reassuring impression.

Rumsfeld: That doesn't mean you need a new institution. No one has mentioned the Arms Control and Disarmament Agency, which was established by Congress for the specific purpose of having some institutional focus on a continuing basis on the issues of arms control and disarmament.

   Now, as a practical matter, it's not surprising no one's mentioned it. As an institution, it has not been able to do very much because, in fact, the fundamental responsibilities lie first with the president and, as Al properly said, with the secretary of state and the secretary of defense. For the Congress to simply add a new institution and give it a nice label—Agency for Arms Control and Disarmament or Department of Peace—does not make the world more peaceful. The task is to make our present institutions work better, more successfully.

Bill Otterson: I'll direct this to General Goodpaster because he's had twenty-five-years' experience in observing it. With regards to the Soviet Union, in your opinion, what is the reason for the Soviet Union's build-up in military capability to such an incredible strength?

Chancellor: I'm going to raise an objection to that. This is a conference on how you run the White House. If you can figure out a way to ask that question within the context of how the White House is run, then I think you can raise that question.

Goodpaster: John, how about, How does a president organize his staff to deal with a question of that kind, and what process does he use to deal with it? I'll cite the process used during the particular administration that I'm familiar with.

Eisenhower, in early 1953, set up a study group consisting of three teams. This is called a solarium study, and each team was charged with evaluating a line of policy in light of their interpretation of the Soviet Union, its policies and actions. Each team was charged with making the best possible case for that particular line of policy. One of the policies was rollback, which had been greatly discussed during the campaign; the second was containment, which had grown out of George Kennan's contributions; and the third was drawing a line identifying spheres of interest, spheres of influence around the world.[8]

---

8. The policy of "rollback" or "liberation" regarding Soviet domination of Eastern Europe was put forth by members of the Eisenhower administration who wanted to differentiate their policies from those of President Truman. The "spheres of influence" formulation was never publicly proposed since it implied Western acquiescence to communist control of Eastern Europe and acceptance of a divided Germany. The most efficacious U.S. position, politically and militarily, remained that of containment, initially espoused by President Truman. An article written by George Kennan, but published under the signature "Mr. X" in *Foreign Affairs*

These three teams worked for about five weeks and they came in and presented to Eisenhower and the top people in government their findings and their best shot, their best case for each one of those lines of policy. The president had all the leaders of government present, and each in the presence of all heard all of this. And at the end he jumped up, as George Kennan described it later, and called George back to head up the team on containment. As George described it, the president analyzed what had been offered and then came down on a line of policy which really was to be the central line of policy for the rest of his administration.

That's the procedure that he used, and I can just tell you that part of the assessment could be captured in a comment from Winston Churchill concerning the Soviets: "They seek the fruits of war without the costs of war."

Sorensen: I would just add that Andy's interpretation of that question raises probably the most controversial issue in White House staffing and one that we barely touched on today. That is the role of the national se-

---

(July 1947), served as the basis for the Truman Doctrine, which pledged to resist communist expansion around the world.

Kennan viewed the sweeping Truman Doctrine as an overreaction and subsequently sought to distance himself from its open-ended military commitments. When the Soviets invaded Hungary in 1956, the U.S. and Western Europe chose not to risk a war with Moscow to challenge the political status quo. See Joseph M. Jones, *The Fifteen Weeks* (New York: Viking, 1955), p. 252; A. W. DePorte, *Europe Between the Superpowers: The Enduring Balance* (New Haven: Yale University Press, 1979), pp. 126–29.

curity advisor.[9] If there's been a subject that has caused fights in Washington over these last two dozen years, it has been the question of whether there should be one and what his role should be. Let me follow your example, John, and give some quick yes-or-no answers.

Should there be a national security advisor to the president even though we have secretaries of state and defense? Yes.

Should he make policy to the extent, say, that Henry Kissinger did when Bill Rogers was secretary of state? No.

Should he be making declarations of national policy the way Brzezinski did when Vance was secretary of state? No.

Should he and his staff be conducting operations the way the present national security staff has conducted operations in Nicaragua? No.

Watson: I agree with every one of those answers.

Chancellor: We have now had the Sorensen Doctrine, which I must say I find absolutely persuasive, but

---

9. The position of special assistant to the president for national security affairs was created during Eisenhower's first term. During its early years, this advisor's role was strictly subordinate to the secretary of state and involved coordinating the flow of foreign affairs information into the White House. For a summary history of the emergence and evolution of this office, see Anna Kasten Nelson, "National Security I: Inventing a Process (1945–1960)" and I. M. Destler, "National Security II: The Rise of the Assistant (1961–1981)" in Hugh Heclo and Lester M. Salamon (eds.), *The Illusion of Presidential Government* (Boulder, Colo.: Westview Press, 1981), pp. 229–87.

let's see about the others. I'd just like to go around the table here.

Rumsfeld: I quite agree, you have to have a national security advisor to bring those threads up between the Central Intelligence Agency and—but I do not think he ought to be making public pronouncements, and I do not think it's the responsibility of White House staff to conduct operations.

Watson: I agree.

Goodpaster: I have to say I agree.

McPherson: I wish I could say otherwise, but I agree.

Cheney: Just to make a point or emphasize a point, I agree with what Ted said, and the NSC [National Security Council] spot has been a difficult spot. I think there's a tendency, though, in this area, as there was with the spokes of the wheel. Each new administration tries to organize itself in such a way that it avoids a problem that the previous administration had, but they always misunderstand and get it wrong. "Spokes of the wheel" is a classic example of going wrong, and I would argue that the Reagan administration at the outset, in order to avoid the conflict between the NSC advisor and the secretary of state, buried the NSC advisor so far down in the organization that he's totally ineffective.[10]

---

10. In his book *Caveat* Haig confirms Cheney's assessment of Reagan's plans for the national security advisor, then Dick Allen, to "act exclusively as a staff coordinator." Haig writes: "With a quick glance to Dick Allen, Reagan repeated his desire that his National Security Advisor should be a staff man, not a man of policy or spokes-

I would argue, too, that the NSC advisor performs a very useful role in part because everybody else— with one or two exceptions, the chief of staff and one or two others—everybody in the White House, everybody in the administration, is a specialist. The secretary of state—maybe Al would disagree with me— the secretary of state has parochial interests. He looks at the globe and looks at it from the standpoint of State, not Civil Defense, or CIA, or one of the other agencies.

The national security advisor is in a position to bring to all the internal debate and controversy that's bound to reign between those departments the kind of a broad, generalist view that only the president shares, and it is vital to have. It would be a very strong position, to avoid the pitfalls that Ted's talked about.

Haig: I agree with all the observations that have been made, but I do make a point that it can work either way. If the president decides he wants a national security advisor to be the focal point of our national security policy, then it will work. I would prefer that it not be that way. He can pick the doorman at the White House, as a matter of fact. Jack Kennedy, to a large extent, gave his brother, the attorney general of the United States, amazing authority to coordinate the conduct of foreign policy. I know. I was part of the mechanism. So it works.

---

man. If Allen had any quibble with this concept, he said nothing about it to the President on this occasion or to me at any time before or after." Haig, *Caveat,* p. 58.

But the point that I think can be drawn from all of this is that while it's not in the Constitution, it has become executive fiat and tradition that the cabinet officer who is confirmed, who sits on top of a huge bureaucracy with tentacles all over the world, really is the best fellow to be the principal man on the conduct of foreign policy, not defense policy.

In the two-party system we have, the Democratic party has generally believed in an above-the-cabinet-level role for the secretary of state. They have looked to him to coordinate all the defense or security-related agencies in behalf of the president. The Republican party has generally believed that the buck stops at the president's desk and he is responsible. So this is theory.

But if you go back into the Jackson subcommittee hearings of 1959, '60, '61, all these things were discussed.[11] You'll find the Republicans testifying that the president must be strong, must have a strong national security advisor; the Democrats were suggesting that secretary of state should be the vicar. That's a dirty word. So I tell you, it works either way, in my experience, and I've been on teams where both of them were operating.

Sorensen: But if it's going to work Al Haig's way, then the national security advisor should be confirmed by the

11. In the wake of *Sputnik* and the bogus "missile gap," Senator Henry ("Scoop") Jackson's subcommittee on national policy machinery heard testimony from scores of witnesses in and out of government regarding all aspects of U.S. security and defense. Particular attention was given to the quality of information and advice available to the president.

Senate and should be subject to subpoena by the Congress, which gets into all kinds of questions of executive privilege, to mention another dirty word, that I'd rather not get into.

Haig: That's why I prefer a strong role for the secretary of state, but not a stronger capability.

Controlling information—and misinformation?

Frank Gormley: I'd like to ask a question relating to the costs of the White House staff, the costs in terms of democracy. Mr. Sorensen, I'd like to ask what you think about the way the White House staff was used during the 1972 presidential election, precisely during the time that we call the Watergate conspiracy and cover-up. Do you think that the Constitution was usurped, that democracy was set aside perhaps temporarily for a White House Nixon dictatorship?

The second part of my question is directed to Mr. Haldeman. Are there any lessons you have to give your current counterparts in manipulating the media, in misinforming the American public on how to successfully run a war in a third-world country? Thank you.

Sorensen: I won't necessarily endorse all the wording of the question addressed to me. It is in the Constitution that the president is impeachable for high crimes and misdemeanors. The Judiciary Committee of the House of Representatives found that the conduct and the cover-up involved in Watergate and associated errors fulfilled that constitutional standard of high crimes and misdemeanors, and I certainly agree with their conclusion.[12]

I might add, I think the Constitution worked in the case of Watergate. It was not a failure of the Constitution. It was a great victory for the Constitution.

Chancellor: Any other comments from members of the panel?

Haig: This reminds me of one of the last cabinet meetings I attended. (*Laughter*)

Chancellor: I think we have to go on. I'm not sure we are going to shed a lot of light on this.

Doug Newhart: As White House chief of staff, you control the influx of information to the president in a very specific way. You allow some things to go through and some things not to go through, and you are also a trusted personal advisor to the president. How

---

12. On July 27, 1974, the House Judiciary Committee approved two articles of impeachment against President Nixon, one for obstructing justice and another for violating his oath of office. Six days later they adopted a third article of impeachment, this for the defiance of congressional committee subpoenas. Nixon resigned on August 9; on September 17 President Ford granted Nixon an unconditional pardon. Members of Nixon's inner circle who were convicted of crimes associated with the scandals include H. R. Haldeman (chief of staff), John D. Ehrlichman (chief domestic advisor), John N. Mitchell (attorney general), John W. Dean (White House legal counsel), and Egil Krogh, Jr. (White House aide).

much influence do you believe your personal opinions had on the president, especially in policy decision making in urgent matters where he doesn't have a lot of time or a lot of people to consult. Also, what's your criteria for limiting information that reaches the president?

Goodpaster: That's a very interesting premise that you put forward, that the chief of staff, who was Governor Sherman Adams, or I, or the staff secretary, or anybody controlled the flow of information to President Eisenhower. I can tell you that did not happen. He controlled the flow of information, and he had his outside sources, beyond the organized process, providing information to him. That, of course, is one of the powers of the president, and he's not about to turn that power over to anybody.[13]

Eisenhower didn't want a flood of irrelevant information coming in. But you were allowed—as he had told me one time in January, he said, "I allow each of my staff to make one mistake a year. You have had yours." (*Laughter*)

Over a period of time, and it doesn't take very long, you come to understand the kind of thing that he wants to come to him and the kind of thing he does

---

13. While President Eisenhower reserved the prerogative to intervene at any stage of staff deliberation, he insisted on organizational routines that would leave him the choice of endorsing or rejecting largely finished policies. For descriptions of Eisenhower's organizational style, see Stephen Hess, *Organizing the Presidency* (Washington, D.C.: Brookings Institution, 1976), pp. 59–77; Fred I. Greenstein, *The Hidden-Hand Presidency: Eisenhower as Leader* (New York: Basic Books, 1982).

not want to come to him because he thinks somebody else should handle it, or it simply is not worth part of the precious twenty-four hours a day of the president.

Cheney: That's a key point. I think the key thing is to separate out the two roles.

Oftentimes, I think when you sit outside the White House, you assume the chief of staff is sitting there making these decisions to sort of keep information away from the president. But my experience was similar to General Goodpaster's. That doesn't happen. You carry a lot of information *in* to them.

You may carry in a package of memos that he will read before he vetoes or signs a bill, before he makes a key decision. He will often ask you what you think on that issue and you tell him. But you make certain he understands when you are giving him your own opinion and when you are passing on the opinions of those in the administration with whom he wants to consult before he makes a decision.

I don't think you have a situation where a chief of staff survives very long if he, in effect, warps the flow of information to suit his own bias with respect to policy. Then he's not serving the interest of the president. It's very easily found out after two or three times, and it seems to me that anybody who did that would quickly find himself going down the road.

Haldeman: If the chief of staff, or the staff secretary, or anybody else in the staff organization, as you put it, "controls" the information that goes to the president in terms of the physical process of getting paper to the president or bringing paper back from the president, that exercise is done in the role of an honest broker if the chief of staff is worth a damn. And if he isn't, he isn't going to be there very long, as Dick said.

He functions as an honest broker in the sense of eliminating or bringing together repetitious material, of making sure that opposing material is also available when one side of an issue is presented, and organizing the material in an orderly manner so that the president can proceed through it. The president shouldn't have ten piles of irrelevant or unrelated paper that he's got to wade through, sort out, and figure out what to do with. That's the staff's function.

The president's function is to take all that information and make the decision on the basis of that. The whole effort that the White House staffperson responsible for that area is making every minute of his working day is to ensure that the president is making the right decisions for the right reasons. That means getting the right information to him on all sides of an issue, along with the recommendations of those advisors from whom the president wants recommendations on that particular issue.

Rumsfeld: The answer to the question about what influence any of the various chiefs of staff have had on their presidents is: exactly what the president wanted.

Chancellor: No Svengalis.

Rumsfeld: No.

Fred Greenstein: Let me pose the notion that a staff sometimes works better and sometimes worse. You all agreed that the staff has to fit the president's needs. Suppose we think of those needs in terms of the strengths and weaknesses that these six presidents had. Could a few of you offer illustrations of a presidential strength that was augmented by good staffing, or a presidential strength that was blunted because the staffing really wasn't up to the president's needs? And take the fascinating flip side of it, a presidential weakness that was perhaps compensated for by good staffing, or worse yet, a presidential weakness magnified by unsatisfactory staffing.

Chancellor: Some of the panelists here have said, "Gee, we would like to think overnight about that one." (*Laughter*) But let me see if I can prod them a little bit.

General Goodpaster, you were a senior member of the White House staff, very influential, when President Eisenhower had a series of very serious illnesses. Addressing ourselves to the question of how staff support can be used, During his illnesses, when he was unable to run the country, what did you do?[14]

Goodpaster: Let me refer here to Bill Hopkins, the chief clerk, who was tremendously valuable to all of us in our successive times.

---

14. On September 24, 1955, President Eisenhower suffered a heart attack. Eisenhower remained in an army hospital outside Denver until November 11, and he did not return to the White House until January 1956. During that time, Sherman Adams and John Foster Dulles assumed many of the burdens of the presidency. In mid-February Eisenhower's doctors pronounced him recovered, and he declared his intention to seek reelection. On November 25, 1957, Eisenhower suffered a mild stroke but maintained a full schedule.

As soon as we learned of the president's illness, Bill came to us and he said, "Now, there are many, many things that can be done here," and he knew from the man with whom he had worked in Hoover's time, who himself had been there during Woodrow Wilson's time. He knew some of the things that could be done and could properly be done, and some of the things that would be improper to do. One thing we did was sort out the material that had to be dealt with according to the time when a decision would be needed.

Another thing we did was to get the facts together in a way that would be brief so that the president, as Bill Hopkins put it, by a simple nod of the head could let us know whether something was acceptable to him or whether he wanted more work done on it. That's how we worked with President Eisenhower, taking material to him and presenting it to him in that way. We organized it according to our notion of time and checked to see whether that was his notion of urgency.

Chancellor: And he would nod his head?

Goodpaster: He would nod his head or sign a paper when a signature was needed.

His heart attack came at a time—it was on September 24, 1955—at a time when there was no pressing pending legislation. So we had a little more latitude, a little more elbow room. Once he had gone up to Gettysburg to begin his recuperation, either Governor Adams or myself flew up there every day, or went up by car when the weather was bad, to take up these things with him and see that he was satisfied.

We finally arranged a session so that he could meet with the cabinet, so that he could meet with the National Security Council. You can do a great deal in focusing the issue in just that way.

Chancellor: The meetings must not have taken very long.

Goodpaster: We would have quite a number of issues. And if you knew Eisenhower, you knew that he wasn't going to be satisfied with nodding. He would be telling you, "I want information on this. I want you to get so-and-so looking into this," and so on. That was the theory, that was the basis of it, and beyond that, it was really up to him and between him and his doctors as to what he would decide to do.

Chancellor: That's a fascinating story. I never heard that.

Rumsfeld: From a slightly different slant, when President Nixon resigned and suddenly Vice-President Ford was president, Al Haig was chief of staff for President Nixon and continued for President Ford. President Ford brought me back in as chairman of this transition.

I don't know if the other participants in that transition would all agree with me, but my impression was that the main focus was on the work of the government, the things that needed to be done. Ford, using his natural instincts, did a lot of things that didn't really fit what the staffs were urging him to do in terms of using his time. But in the last analysis, Ford's basic human decency and comfortableness with himself, I think, did a great deal to replenish that reservoir of trust in the United States that had been drained. It wasn't anything that the staff organized, really. It was more just Gerald Ford as a human being.

Would you agree with that, Al?

Haig: Very much so. I would say also, we have talked about image makers around our current president. The facts are that these fellows have been very effective. But without them, I've seen him rise to every occasion due to his natural, personal instincts which break through.

Riding the popularity roller coaster

Samuel Kernell: With the exception of General Goodpaster, all of you gentlemen had the privilege of serving under presidents who have shown an uncanny capacity to lose the public's support. What is that like within the White House? How does the president's unpopularity—whether it comes quickly, as with Ford, or slowly, as with Johnson—reverberate through the White House? Does it trigger an organizational response or just create a different morale or climate within the White House?

Chancellor: Do you mean a ten-point drop in the Gallup popularity rating, the job approval rating?

Kernell: That's a good scenario to play with.

Chancellor: Let's start with Jack Watson. What happens? Panic? Diving out the windows? President's down ten colossal points.

Watson: With us, it was usually twenty-five. (*Laughter and applause*) I can honestly say that it doesn't really affect your performance of your duties in terms of your professional approach to getting done that day what you need to get done. Most of my colleagues in the Carter White House, members of the cabinet, were professionals in a really positive, powerful sense of that word. They had jobs to do, duties to perform, and they did them.

Where it hits you, and hits you in a very real way, is in your morale. Everyone who works for the president identifies closely with him. His successes, you share in. His failures, his gaffes, his stumbles—

Rumsfeld: His lusts. (*Laughter*)

Watson: What happens to a White House staff when the president's down in the polls? A combination of things. Sometimes there's a renewed vigor to pull together, analyze what it is that's killing us and try to do something about it. Sometimes there are external events over which you have absolutely no control, the taking by the Iranians of the American hostages, for example.

One thing that President Carter did there that I thought at the time was a terrible mistake—and I said so, but my advice was not taken—was his decision to announce to the American public that he was not going to leave the White House [to campaign for reelection] until the hostages were back. I did not think it was a good decision. I thought it tied him too closely to the event—not that he wasn't tied emotionally, mentally, and in every other way to it, not that he wasn't on top of it every day. But I thought that that continuing reverberating—I never will forget every night just cringing, listening to Walter Cronkite on the CBS News, "It's the 147th day . . ."

So there are events you can't control: the Iranian situation with the American hostages, or the oil crisis, when OPEC raised its benchmark price and oil prices increased by 12 percent a month for a period of twelve months, between December '79 and December '80. Those kinds of matters you can't control, and you just do the best you can with what you have.

Cheney: There's a key point here when you talk about polls, too, at campaign time that affects the role of the chief of staff. You are in the middle of a presidential campaign. You are getting down to election day, and the polls are up and down. The candidate declares the policy is not dominated by the public opinion and so forth. (*Laughter*)

The chief of staff is the link-up to the president. The president's too busy making speeches. He's out there on the stump being a candidate, so you are the funnel of information to him in terms of how things are going, and you have to keep his mood up. You can't let him get down. You don't lie to him or mislead him, but you have to make certain that everything is going smoothly and that hc knows it's worth the effort.

You are also the reflection of the president for people down in the organization. Everybody in the organization sees a lot more of the chief of staff than they do of the president, and you set the whole tone for the organization. At the back of the plane is the press, and the press plane is behind that, and you are under a spotlight. I felt an enormous responsibility at that point just to send out positive signals to everybody, regardless of the polls, just to keep the organization going, so you have a chance to maybe pull it out.

Chancellor: Kind of a rigid smile at times?

Rumsfeld: Part of the problem, though, is that when things are bad, everything is harder because the Congress starts putting daylight between themselves and the president, and so the work load goes up. Everything gets more difficult as his popularity goes down.

Chancellor: But what I'm trying to get at is this: When the polls dropped swiftly, precipitously, have any of you sat in a meeting and said, "Can we change the way the president behaves?" I'm not saying that you are manipulators of presidential behavior, but in a sense, you are. I mean, you advise him, and you tell him, "Stop telling this particular joke, it doesn't work."

Harry, do you want to talk about that? You see what I'm getting at?

McPherson: No. (*Laughter*) You try everything. Lyndon Johnson had had this terrific roller-coaster ride from '63, from November when he became president, through '64 when I think by very broad, if not universal consent, he performed extremely well in holding the country together, keeping it moving forward in a time of terrible tragedy and national shock.

In '65, when all the Great Society legislation was passed, Congress was working sixty hours a week turning out this enormous spate of legislation and finishing the agenda that had been building up for thirty or forty years. The Congress' own position in the polls was extremely high. The country liked the way everything was working. They liked the hard-working president, hard-working Congress. Things were going very well. The economy was in good shape, inflation was low; Vietnam had not become the animal that it was to become.

By '66 things were sliding. From then on, you began thinking very sharply and keenly every day of what you might do to tinker with this or that. "Shall we use a teleprompter? Shall we not use a teleprompter? Should the president look more formal and stiff in the attempt to be a leader or shall he be himself?" Several of us thought he should be that, he ought to really be—

Rumsfeld: Show his scar.

McPherson: Sure. "Why don't you show them the scar?"[15] (*Laughter*) I've listened with great understanding and a sense of poignancy to Jack talking about President Carter. When these things catch up, when OPEC price rises are going up 100 percent a year, there isn't anything you can do about it, really.

---

15. Shortly after an appendectomy, President Johnson showed his scar to reporters at a press conference, an act that garnered him a measure of ridicule. A *Newsweek* editor asked Johnson's special consultant John Roche, "Why the hell did Johnson show his scar?" Roche's response was reported in the next week's issue: "One thing that we should really be happy about is that he wasn't operated on for hemorrhoids." Such incidents secured this anecdote's place in the pantheon of Johnson stories. See John P. Roche, "Comments on Part VI," in Marc Landy (ed.), *Modern Presidents and the Presidency* (Lexington, Mass.: Lexington Books, 1985), pp. 187–91.

You can launch an attack, I suppose, but people wouldn't want you to do that. And when your diplomats are in the compound in Teheran, you can't do anything about that. You try, and then this awful symbol of American weakness, the failure of smoking helicopters in the desert, just makes it all the worse.

Franklin Roosevelt, with that situation, or Ronald Reagan, in that situation, would have been hard-pressed to cope. I suspect they could have coped better than either Carter or Johnson because they were simply better, to use that boring phrase, communicators. They were better at it, and they could better speak out their own view. But, boy, it's a tough one when those polls are sliding down. Everybody looks good and feels good when they are going up, but you have a terrible time when your boss is going down.

Chancellor: On that note, questioners, audience, faculty, thank you very much. That brings us to the end of this session.

★ **3** ★

Quarterback, Cheerleader, or Javelin Catcher?

The third session of the conference was designed to give invited scholars and journalists an opportunity to explore in more detail issues raised at the preceding sessions. Invited to serve as chief questioners were Richard E. Neustadt and David S. Broder. Mr. Neustadt, professor of public administration, JFK School of Government, Harvard University, is the author of *Presidential Power: The Politics of Leadership from FDR to Carter*; during the 1960s he served as a consultant to presidents Kennedy and Johnson, and to the State Department. Mr. Broder is a columnist and editor at the *Washington Post* and author of *Changing of the Guard: Power and Leadership in America*; in 1973 he received a Pulitzer Prize for journalistic commentary.

The other participants in this session are identified in the introductory note to the second session, except for Jim Squires, editor of the *Chicago Tribune*; Arnold Kanter, of the Rand Corporation; and Gerald Warren, editor of the *San Diego Union*, deputy press secretary for presidents Nixon and Ford, and the chief organizer of the conference.

Due to other commitments, Alexander Haig and Harry McPherson were not present at this session, held on the morning of January 18, 1986.

Kernell: This morning we are here to review some of the issues that were covered yesterday, perhaps to reflect more broadly upon the implications of the observations and insights that you gentlemen have shared with us. We've asked David Broder and Richard E. Neustadt to each make some opening remarks, perhaps to set an agenda for this session. David, would you like to begin?

Politics and the White House staff

David Broder: Sure. It was a fascinating day yesterday. I thought the discussion about crisis management, which is a field I don't know beans about, was probably very important for that subject. I thought that we heard some wonderful stories and were able vicariously to share the camaraderie among the eight of you and sensible comments about the administration of the White House, and what I thought was very good constitutional doctrine on the notion of the disadvantages of confirmation of White House staff people.

I thought we heard surprisingly little about the exercise of power in personal terms and about the practice of politics in institutional terms. That omission bothered me some as a journalist, because Jim Squires and I and our colleagues spend an awful lot of time, maybe too much time, writing about and focusing on the political role of the White House staff. Maybe that's a misguided focus on our part. Wouldn't be the first time.

But, to be candid, I was somewhat skeptical about some of the denial that I thought I was hearing yesterday. I don't think I've heard such sincere and such unconvincing denials since the last time I heard myself talking about the role of the press—(*Laughter*)—we get also very defensive about any notion that we are perhaps exercising influence or power.

I looked around that semicircle and I saw some people who, in other times, in other places, had discussed in guarded terms the political plots in which they were engaged, plots against Congress to get it to do what they wanted it to do, plots against the cabinet, corporate or individual, to thwart some of their goals or help them carry them forward, plots against the bureaucracy, constant efforts to try to get them to behave, and from time to time, plots against the president himself to get him to do or not do something that those staff people thought he should or should not be doing. And except for Harry McPherson, who is not here this morning, I didn't hear very many people acknowledging that it was really a political function that they were playing in the White House staff. I'd like to hear more talk about that.

A couple of specific suggestions as to areas that I hope we will explore. I'd like to know about how you folks dealt with the strong cabinet members in your time. I'd like to know whether you would really maintain that you were simply honest brokers when it came to carrying forward the wishes of weak cabinet members. Would you, for example, deny that you had perhaps more power than the secretary of commerce in your time?

I'd like to know about the chief of staff's relationship with the Senate and House leaders of the president's party. Did you deal with them, and if so, on what terms? I'd also like to hear about your relationships with the vice-presidents.

Rumsfeld: Who?

Haldeman: Scratch that one.

Broder: There are people here who, by reputation, programmed the vice-president to say or do certain things. There are people here who punished the vice-president for doing or saying certain things. There are people here who, in one or two instances, maybe even made the vice-president disappear. I'd like to know how they did that and why they did that.

Kernell: Thanks, now let's hear from Dick Neustadt.

Richard Neustadt: First, I've been waiting for an opportunity to make a confession to Jack Watson. For years I tried to hold open the possibility that presidents could have White House staffs small enough so they never had to designate anybody as the administrative coordinator of the staff itself.

In that respect, I think I gave Jack worse advice than Dick Cheney did. He and Rumsfeld had experienced the effort to reduce the White House staff— that is, people who have some substantive responsibility, not the clerical workers and all that—to a size small enough to be comparable to, say, Kennedy's time or Truman's time, and they had not succeeded.

I think that was a real effort, and I think they probably got it down to the smallest size possible, but even at that minimum you do need some administrative coordinator. So that to leave open the option of letting the president be his own administrative coordinator was probably unrealistic in '76, and I'm sorry, Jack. Not that I think it would have made any difference. (*Laughter*)

I looked around the table, too, and several things occurred to me. Most of those who spoke yesterday had had previous experience of government and in Washington, but two had not. I'd be very interested in some comparative talk about what it's like to take on a major White House role without previous Washington experience or government experience. What are the relative advantages and disadvantages of experience?

Watching White Houses, I've noticed that most of the time, chief of staff or no chief of staff, whatever the designation or title, there's a "big three" or a "big three to five." This certainly goes back to FDR. It's true of Truman's time; it's true of Eisenhower's; it's true of yours, Ted. Three people who are more equal than others. You can say that about Kennedy's term and Ronald Reagan's first term and most of the White Houses in between. You can say it right up until the first year of Mr. Reagan's second term, and that raises an interesting question for me.

I was charmed to see how much solidarity there was among you, even, one might almost say, chivalry among you, which means, I think, that it is a very professionalizing experience to have been one of those three senior staff members. But there's something about the experience that does not seem to be readily communicable to people who haven't been there. Else, how could Don Regan have conducted himself the way he's conducted himself in his first year? I'd like to hear about the transition problem, whether anything can be done to wise up people faster when they take on these roles.

Finally, listening, I thought a little bit about the absent members of this circle, the presidents. I once had a very sobering experience hearing Harry Truman describe the work of my boss, Charlie Murphy, to Adlai Stevenson when Stevenson had first been nominated. Truman, though he knew nobody could beat Eisenhower, was trying to be gallant, attend Stevenson, though he didn't think he was going to be president. Truman described Murphy's job to Stevenson: "Here's my lawyer," he said. "He fools around with enrolled bills and executive orders, gives me legal advice and things like that." Well, Murphy was Clifford's successor and sort of the nearest thing there was to a Sorensen at the time.[1] It was not the way I'd

---

1. Clark Clifford served as naval aide to Truman in 1946, and from 1946 to 1950 as his special counsel. Charles Murphy served Truman first as administrative assistant from 1947 to 1950 and from 1950 to 1953 as special counsel.

have described the job, but it may very well have been the way Truman thought of it.

It's not clear to me that presidents look upon senior staffs with the seriousness the senior staffs look at the senior staffs, and I'd appreciate some discussion of that.

Kernell: Ted, of the remarks that Dave and Dick offered, are there certain things that you would like to begin the discussion with?

Sorensen: Of course, I'd like to comment on all of them. Let me just go through some of them very quickly.

I remember, Dave, in the early days of the Johnson administration when I stayed on, as I mentioned, for three months, there was quite a bit of talk by staff members about power, using the word *power*. I was struck by it because in the Kennedy White House, we never talked about power and John F. Kennedy rarely ever talked about power. It seemed to me that those who are comfortable in the exercise of power don't talk about it a lot, and those who are new to it or uncomfortable with it may talk about it more. The reason the eight of us did not talk about it in those terms yesterday may have been because having been in that spot in the White House, we were comfortable with it. Power is what we were talking about all the time without having to describe it as power or exalt it as power.

Were we performing political functions? Of course we were, from beginning to end. The presidency is a political office. I don't make any apology for that. It's intended to be a political office, and the president's senior staff must keep politics in mind at all times.

I'm talking about politics in its broadest sense, not necessarily partisan or even presidential politics, but politics in the sense of bearing in mind how far out in front of the country you can move. The president must always keep in mind a host of multiple constituencies, the Congress, the bureaucracies, and the interest groups. In that sense, politics was always on our minds, and I think properly so.

How did we deal with strong cabinet members? I'm sure each of us would have a different story to tell. I had a different kind of strong cabinet member because he was the president's brother, and he was not willing to submit his legislative plans and policies to my office as the other cabinet members did. But over a period of time, he began to realize that coordination made more sense than parallel actions, and we worked quite closely together.

Popkin: Why did he realize that?

Sorensen: Why did he realize that? Because I think he found that there were some values in working with our office. We had some wisdom to bring to bear. He was a part of the president's team. The president was trying to put forward a legislative package or a coherent policy, and the actions of the Justice Department had to be a part of that, not going off on their own. Also, I think, frankly, Robert Kennedy, as a personality, was evolving during those three years, and he and I got along better all the time.[2]

---

2. Victor S. Navasky has explored the ramifications for the Department of Justice of having the president's brother serve as attor-

Berman: Why was President Kennedy more comfortable in using power? I don't really follow that.

Sorensen: I was talking about the Johnson aides in the early months as compared with the Kennedy aides, not Johnson compared with Kennedy.

Cheney: Just to follow up on the comment on strong cabinet members. You haven't dealt with a strong cabinet member until you've dealt with a Henry Kissinger, who is not only secretary of state but also national security advisor. Several of us, I think, had experience with this.

That was a special problem during Nixon's term, frankly, and eventually President Ford made the decision, after he had been there for about a year, that this super-powerful cabinet member, Henry, would lose his second hat as head of the National Security Council. That was, I think, a significant decision for the president to make, something he wrestled with a long time before he finally decided that that was the right way to go.

---

ney general. Although his special access to the Oval Office facilitated Robert Kennedy's efforts to direct the Justice Department's (and to a lesser degree the FBI's) energies to pet projects, including a concerted drive against organized crime, Navasky offers evidence that Attorney General Kennedy frequently shied away from conflict with FBI Director J. Edgar Hoover out of concern for the political costs that might redound to the president. Not until Johnson was in the White House was Robert Kennedy willing to spend the president's political capital in an effort to regain control of the FBI, which under Hoover had become a semi-autonomous agency. Navasky, *Kennedy Justice* (New York: Atheneum, 1971).

But if you looked at it from the perspective of the chief of staff, the problem continuously was that while you wanted the enormous expertise that Henry had and his intellect and his ability and everything he stood for—and he was important in terms of the continuity and policy from the Nixon to the Ford administration, that is, that President Nixon's resignation did not mean a change in policy. By the same token, there's a constant worry, I think a legitimate one, that the president is not getting credit for foreign policy; Henry Kissinger is getting credit for foreign policy.

Popkin: Can you give an example, just an anecdote, of how it helped you and the president after Henry was no longer NSC head?

Cheney: You still were able to draw upon the enormous talent that Henry brought to the job, but there was at least the appearance, and I think partly the reality, too, that the president was less the captive of a single advisor.

Popkin: Are you saying that this is all outside the White House, the same policy with more credit for the president, or somehow the policy was going to be different with an NSC—

Cheney: It was less a matter of the policy being different—Kissinger still dominated foreign policy questions—and more a perception that in fact, the president was in charge of foreign policy. That oftentimes wasn't the perception when Henry controlled everything, NSC as well as the State Department.

"Personality" conflicts

Cheney: The other problem you run into, that we ran into repeatedly, is when you have a major conflict between two willful cabinet members. I can't count the number of times I would get a phone call, probably about once a month, and it would be a situation in which Pat Moynihan was calling threatening to resign or Henry Kissinger was threatening to resign because they didn't like each other. Of course, Pat was ambassador to the U.N. and Henry was at State.[3]

I remember the bicentennial celebration at the House of Burgesses in Williamsburg, Virginia. Very hot day in July. The president was delivering a major address where Patrick Henry had spoken two hundred years before, and I was in the closet upstairs on the White House telephone with Pat Moynihan trying one more time to keep Pat from resigning because Henry had said something about him that had been

---

3. During this period, Daniel P. Moynihan served as the U.S. ambassador to the United Nations. As early as January 1976, Moynihan had publicly campaigned against what he believed to be State Department efforts to undermine his confrontational tactics in the United Nations. Secretary of State Kissinger and others suggested that perhaps Moynihan's behavior was motivated by an upcoming bid for a Senate seat rather than by a concern with furthering U.S. interests in the General Assembly. That November Moynihan was indeed elected to the Senate. See Leslie H. Gelb, "Moynihan Says State Department Fails to Back Policy Against U.S. Foes in U.N.," *New York Times*, January 28, 1976.

printed in Scotty Reston's column.[4] I think all of us had that experience at one time or another, probably all with Moynihan. (*Laughter*)

Jim Squires: Dick, those are important events inside the White House, and they become very important events to the people who cover the White House. In fact, I think such events may dominate the press maneuvering in an administration—that is what Dave was talking about when we started, the exercise of a chief of staff's power in the political interest of the president, particularly within the interworkings and rivalries of the administration.

I wonder, after all these years of covering those events and talking to many of you about them at the time, how White Houses, in the best interest of their president, should communicate those episodes to the American people. Those episodes tend to be kept secret. We know that Henry Kissinger does not like Pat Moynihan only because he tells Scotty Reston. We know that Pat Moynihan is upset about that because he tells David Broder. But we never know up front whether Bob Haldeman or Dick Cheney is intimately involved and is actively trying to do something to resolve the problem. Generally, the press remains in the dark about the chief of staff's role there.

I think what Dave was talking about is that the impression one would have gotten yesterday is that you all are a rather passive group, that basically all

---

4. James ("Scotty") Reston joined the *New York Times* in 1939. Since 1960 he has written a thrice-weekly column, now syndicated, on politics and government.

you do is go in and tell the president, "Henry's mad at Pat, Pat's mad at Henry, and what should we do about this, sir?"

Cheney: Well, you try to solve the problem for the president. Of course, it may end up on his desk if you can't resolve the differences between those giant egos.

Popkin: What were you allowed to do for Pat? Give him a ride on Air Force One, use of the White House Mess, I mean, tennis lessons? What would you do for him?

Cheney: Sometimes it would be a matter of "it's time for a little presidential stroking," okay? You're going to have a cabinet meeting next week. You say, "Pat, the president would like to see you afterwards," and you get him in for a fifteen- or twenty-minute chat in the Oval Office, and the president tells him how important he is to the policy of his administration. It's that kind of operation more than the byzantine plotting, "Well, let's see. If I go over here and I leak something to Broder and it will run here and this guy will react." That doesn't happen. At least it didn't happen on our watch in my job. I'm sure there were others who were doing that kind of thing, but basically it's a matter of trying to manage that operation for the president at the point.

The press has a major weakness: it can't cover very effectively policy differences. It's very easy to cover personality conflicts, which you guys are guilty of all the time. I don't mean you personally, Jim. What the press is dealing out all the time is cheapening the dialogue and the debate that takes place over fundamental differences of policy. If you've got a strong secretary of state who wants to go one way and a strong secretary of defense who wants to go the other way, it's reported as a Weinberger-Schultz conflict, instead of an analysis of whatever merit there might be in the two policy positions.

Squires: What's wrong with being as candid in the press room or on "Meet the Press" as you are in this room now? Just say "Jeane Kirkpatrick hates Al Haig and Al Haig hates Jeane Kirkpatrick, and the reason they do is that they have these differences in policy and they are at odds for the president's approval here," instead of all of the backroom maneuvering and "no comments."[5]

Cheney: The headline, Jim, that comes out of that kind of briefing in the White House press corps is: White House Press Secretary Announces Chaos in the Administration. (*Laughter*)

Squires: I feel that people who make the decisions about when we go public, when we do not, and what we tell the press, underestimate the intelligence of the American people. Wouldn't we be better off if we acknowledged personnel differences and firings in a very open fashion rather than going through all of the charades? You go through them and we go through them, and as a result, we don't get to the policy. We deal with the charade.

---

5. Jeane J. Kirkpatrick was U.S. ambassador to the United Nations from 1981 to early 1985. She and Haig feuded over the nature and implementation of American foreign policy. In one instance, Haig's aides openly criticized Kirkpatrick's handling of negotiations on a U.N. resolution condemning an Israeli air strike against an Iraqi nuclear installation.

Haldeman: Jim, you are suggesting that the way to solve a marital problem is for both members of the couple to discuss with the neighbors every fight that they have and make sure that the neighbors understand why there was all that shouting coming out of the house. That's not going to resolve anything.

The way you solve internal problems is internally. If we go back to the question of the role of a chief of staff, my view, as I said yesterday, very strongly, is the passion for anonymity viewpoint. I feel that the chief of staff reports to and works for and works within the president's office. Internal family problems that need to be dealt with within the president's office should be dealt with within the president's office, not in the press room or on the street. When you are dealing with human relations problems, which is exactly what you are talking about, people say things, do things, and think things that are spur of the moment and change at the spur of the next moment, and they can be dealt with.

If you escalate each one of them, if every time Pat Moynihan says he can't stand Henry Kissinger, you put that in the paper, it makes it awfully difficult to work out the next stage of a relationship with Pat Moynihan and Henry Kissinger. I'm only using that example because that's what you said. I had no problem, because in my day Pat Moynihan was the urban affairs counselor and Henry Kissinger was the national security advisor. Their two paths never crossed, and I didn't know they didn't like each other. In fact, at that time, I think they did. They were the only two Harvard professors we had on the staff. (*Laughter*)

My view is that the chief of staff's job is to deal with

those things *within* the White House. I had plenty of
personnel situations to deal with. You didn't hear
about very many of them, and I don't think there
would have been any purpose served nor would anything have been better for your having heard of them
at the time.

You asked why we weren't as candid then as we are
being today. After it's over and it's done, it is valuable
for the academicians, the historians, and the journalists to look back at what happened and why it
happened. While it's happening, you need the privilege of sanctuary to work out those problems before
they are broadcast and can't be worked out.

Squires: Does this take up an inordinate amount of time?

Haldeman: It does.

Squires: I wonder if we don't write those stories as inside
baseball, mainly for the audience of the *Washington
Post* and the audience of the *New York Times*, yet the
fact that those publications deal with that constantly
seems to set an agenda for the rest of the news media.

Haldeman: Well, I think it's pretty titillating stuff, like
all the "what movie star is going out with what other
movie star" kind of stuff. There's some public interest, and from that viewpoint, I guess it's a legitimate
journalistic interest; you are feeding the appetites of
your readers. But I don't think you are serving the
cause of good government, and I think the White
House chief of staff's job is the cause of good government first.

Squires: But from the press standpoint, there is that constant effort to cover up those kinds of problems and

to go through the charades. I think one of the worst times in the Reagan administration, from a publicity point, was that terrible ordeal with President Reagan and Margaret Heckler, trying to sell the American people the idea that "This was a great job we're offering Margaret Heckler and she really loves it."[6] You remember that picture. It sort of says to the American people: "We are going to fool you forever."

Kernell: Just a minute. In the final days of that affair—and it may illustrate a more general point—Margaret Heckler went public; she started drumming up support in Congress. She was quite visible and conspicuous, and her dealings and problems with Donald Regan were reported daily in the press. I think that she escalated the publicity as a way of trying to build support and forestall critics from the White House.

Squires: I think that's true. But what I'm asking is, Why would not a White House chief of staff, say, cut her loose and admit what's going on and decide not to parade the president out with her again in order to try to convince the American people ?

Greenstein: What is your scenario, that they would send her to Ireland and say, "This is a lousy job, we want to dump you on the Irish"? That's ridiculous. (*Laughter*)

---

6. Reportedly pressed by Donald Regan to resign, Secretary of Health and Human Services Heckler battled publicly to keep her post, eventually meeting privately with President Reagan on the issue. Heckler finally resigned and accepted an appointment as ambassador to Ireland.

Squires: No, but the image of the president and [Larry] Speakes and everyone else out trying to smile their way through and not admit that Margaret Heckler has a problem. Why send her to the Irish? Why send her anyplace? If she can be that way, why not just cut her loose and say "Good-bye, Margaret"?

Haldeman: I agree with you. That's what we did with Wally Hickel.[7] It was a disaster, but that's what we did. We cut him loose and we took the heat, and that was that.

Kernell: Of course, you waited until after the 1970 election. (*Laughter*)

Haldeman: We had a rough six months riding it out to the election, I'll tell you.

Rumsfeld: The president leads by persuasion, by consent, not by command, and as you've all said, part of that involves communicating. But communicating means planning out ahead standards as to where you

---

7. On May 6, 1970, two days after four Kent State University students were slain while protesting the administration's Cambodian incursion, Secretary of Interior Walter Hickel wrote to President Nixon imploring him to listen to the youthful protestors. Apparently without authorization, an aide of Hickel's slipped the letter to the newspapers, and Nixon read it, with the rest of the country, on May 7. Shortly thereafter, Nixon decided to remove Hickel. Fearful of the protest that might be stirred up by such an action against this improbable hero of the antiwar movement, the White House opted to wait until after the mid-term elections. On November 23 Hickel was fired along with all six assistant interior secretaries.

are going. To the extent that there's a debate and a discussion, that's healthy; but to the extent that it continues forever and it sends out mis-signals, for example, to the world as to what your policy is or where you are going, it does not contribute to the implementation of whatever policy direction you've started.

It is not surprising that once you have selected a policy you continue to have differences within your cabinet as to how to implement it or whether it was right. But to hype those differences, to constantly go back over them and reanalyze them is a miscommunication once the president has decided on his policy.

The dean of the North Atlantic Treaty Organization when I was over there was Andre de Staercke [ambassador from Belgium], and he made a wonderful comment: "You know, the good Lord gave you skin for a reason. I like to have dinner with you, Don, but I have no desire to watch all your digestive process." The interest of the White House chief of staff is *not* to communicate but ultimately to have government work well, the way the president wants. It requires communicating to do that, but it does not require hyping things that miscommunicate.

You said "Why don't you just say Joe hates Mike and Mike hates Joe?" In fact, they may or may not hate each other, but whatever they think of each other is irrelevant because they have responsibilities and there are legitimate differences between institutions. President Ford got to the point, apparently, with the differences between Schlesinger and Kissinger,[8] not that he was bothered by the differences, though I can't really speak for him because I don't know quite why he did it when he did it. But the public aspects of those differences became apparently intolerable, and Ford reached a point where he called Henry in the office and me in the office and said he was choosing between Kissinger and Schlesinger, and was picking Kissinger. Then he proceeded to put someone in Schlesinger's spot who had basically the same views as Schlesinger—Rumsfeld—who continued the exact same debate within the administration, but not in the press.

The contests were no different. The ones I had to resolve between Kissinger and Schlesinger were no different than the ones Dick was trying to sort through with Brent Scowcroft [Ford's national security advisor] between Rumsfeld and Kissinger. Indeed, in Ford's book, he complained that I was one of the reasons that there wasn't a SALT II agreement.[9] But it was never in the press, and it meant that Ford could, in fact, preside as president and have his direction. Those differences are real and they are not personal. I mean, I don't have anything against Henry. It wasn't that I didn't like Henry, but I had different views on important national issues.

---

8. James Schlesinger served as President Ford's secretary of defense from 1973 to 1975 and as President Jimmy Carter's secretary of energy from 1977 to 1979.
9. President Ford concedes in his memoirs that Donald Rumsfeld, then secretary of defense, and the Joint Chiefs of Staff held trump cards in the White House's efforts to persuade the Senate to ratify the SALT II agreement. Gerald R. Ford, *A Time To Heal* (New York: Harper & Row, 1979), pp. 358–59.

When staff makes a difference

Greenstein: A number of you have talked about how you work as staff with presidents for the ends of good government or, if we want to take the gutsier formulation that Dave Broder began with, how to have political impact and power. Yesterday, one of the main themes was that there were, by and large, no interesting general rules about the mechanics of staff, that each president has his own needs and styles and modes of operation. I'd be interested in circumstances in which staff action has helped prevent the shot in the foot, and instances when, unfortunately, it has augmented the presidential weakness.

Watson: May I take a couple of cracks at this? Before turning to some very specific and hopefully helpful illustrations, a couple of general comments responding to David's comments.

To begin with, I think that the political role of the White House staff is a constant and pervasive function of the staff. I didn't mean to imply, nor am I confident that any of my colleagues was intending to imply, that we didn't do political work every day. Political decisions and the political aspects of what we were doing pervade everything you are dealing with every day.

Kernell: Jack, can you think of examples of one of the more acute political moments of your service to Carter, perhaps with respect to cabinet officials, say, Secretary Califano or someone, where your role was central and you felt that the resolution of conflicts or

issues of personality all depended on your performance? I think that gets to Fred's question as to the
mediating role of staff.

Watson: Let me give a couple of examples, but on the political point, I want to add—and I think this is a para-
phrase, not a quote—President Truman said that
only a good politician can be a good president, words
to that effect. I believe that devoutly. I believe, in fact,
that one of Carter's central problems was that in so
many key ways, he was not a good politician; I would
postulate, a brilliant man, but not a good politician.

Here's an example. One of Carter's greatest weaknesses, I think, which was the flip side of one of his
greatest strengths, was deciding some of the most important things that needed to be done in the interest
of the country and then wanting to get them all done
at once. He was opposed to a lot of the water projects
in the West because he thought they were budget-
busters, and there were great questions about
whether or not they should be funded.[10] He regarded
some of them—I won't debate the wisdom of our
judgment here—but he regarded some of them as
real boondoggles.

For him to take that on during the first year of his
presidency, at the same time that he was doing everything else—economic policy and employment pro-

10. On February 18, 1977, advanced reports of President Carter's plans
to terminate thirty-two water projects were leaked to the press. On
April 18, Carter announced his final list of nineteen projects that
he would recommend be deleted from the budget. "Draining the
Water Projects Out of the Pork Barrel," *National Journal*, April 9,
1977, pp. 540–48.

grams, energy and government reorganization, and all the rest—was folly because it exacerbated his political problem in the West, widened that breach and cut away his congressional support. Ultimately nothing that the staff could do politically could save him, if you will, from his determination to do it all, because he felt that it ought to be done. That was a nonpolitical judgment that he made, in my opinion, and one which caused him great difficulty.

Kernell: Did anyone at that time go in and tell him that Russell Long was chairman of the Senate Finance Committee and that the project being cut was one of his, one in which he had invested a great deal of time and energy?[11] And if Carter ever expected to get hospital cost control, or some of the other legislation through that committee, that Long was the man who could stand in the way?

Watson: Of course we did. Of course we did, and sometimes the president would relent and would negotiate; in fact, the longer he stayed in office, the more he negotiated. I think the Carter—obviously this is something of the highest speculative nature—but I think the Carter of a second term would have, in some significant way, been a different kind of president, a more compromising, a more negotiating kind of president.

---

11. Senator Long and others cited Carter's handling of the water projects as a reason for their lack of enthusiasm for administration proposals. See Haynes Johnson, *In the Absence of Power: Governing America* (New York: Viking, 1980), pp. 159–67.

Popkin: Was there any time when staffing helped to make that happen sooner? Was there anything you staffers could do to try to game this out for him?

Watson: Informing him, informing the president, giving him good information is the way to do that. It's very uncomfortable for me, even with five years of distance, to talk about some of the weaknesses in our own White House staff, but they were there. Some personnel ought to have been changed, and one of the weaknesses of Carter was a loyalty, an admirable, personal loyalty to people who had been with him since the very beginning of his political career in Georgia, or virtually so, people who were slotted in places that they ought not to have been.

There was really only one major public rift, visible to the public and the press, in our cabinet. It was the Secretary Vance–Brzezinski constant turmoil, difference, and the arbiter there was the president himself.[12] That comes close to being a unique situation in which a problem arises because of a senior member of the White House staff who has his daily access to the president. It's not like a rift between two cabinet members, not like a public rift between Pat Moynihan and Henry Kissinger, but a rift between somebody on the inside with regular daily access to the president and a major cabinet officer. Ultimately,

---

12. The "constant turmoil" between Vance and Brzezinski stemmed largely from divergent views of the Soviet Union. An experienced diplomat, Vance sought to broaden areas of cooperation with the Soviets, particularly on arms control. Brzezinski was deeply suspicious of the Russians and continually pressed for an American military build-up to counter Soviet expansionism.

that was something that was permitted by President Carter, in effect, enabled by him, and was resolvable only by him, not by a chief of staff.

Popkin: Did you ever try?

Watson: In my opinion, the way to have resolved that would have been to have replaced Brzezinski. Now, I am an admirer of Zbig. He is a brilliant man, a brilliant man, but he filled the role of a National Security Council advisor in a way that I think, in its definition, was contrary to the best definition of that role. He followed the Kissinger pattern rather than the Brent Scowcroft pattern or, for that matter, the pattern of Bud McFarlane.[13] The problem was ultimately resolvable only by the departure of one of the two of them, and in my judgment, the departure ought to have been Zbig's.

Staff and cabinet

Watson: Let me change tack here a moment and just lay out without much elaboration those things that I was

---

13. Brent Scowcroft and Robert C. ("Bud") McFarlane were assistants to the president for national security affairs in the Nixon/Ford and the Carter White Houses, respectively. The Scowcroft pattern that Watson refers to is one in which the national security advisor defers to the secretary of state; in the Kissinger pattern, the security advisor plays a more independent role.

most frequently working on with the cabinet members.

Budget. The cabinet members are constantly vying with each other for dollars in the budget, the setting of legislative and budget priorities. By and large, the only people who are in a position to reconcile, to the extent that it's possible, or referee those problems are the members of the White House staff. That was an activity in which I was constantly engaged.

Patterson: Not OMB [Office of Management and Budget]?

Watson: Well, OMB is regarded as an adversary, a player with whom the reconciliation must occur.[14] And here again, I come back to my point that a reconciler needs to be a trusted member, an honest broker. Earlier someone asked, Did you *really* act as honest brokers? You always try, because if you don't act as honest brokers, over time, you lose your capability to play, you just ultimately cut yourself out over time.

As secretary to the cabinet for the first part of the administration, for the majority of the administration, my role was to become trusted by the cabinet, so they knew I was not going to double-deal, that I would keep a confidence, that I wasn't going to embarrass them in the press. Over time, you have to

---

14. On the institutional tension between the professionals in the Office of Management and Budget and the president's entourage, see Harold Seidman and Robert Gilmour, *Politics, Position, and Power*, 4th ed. (New York: Oxford University Press, 1986), pp. 67–97. In earlier times, such as during Truman's administration, the president's staff was drawn largely from the ranks of Budget Bureau careerists.

build that trust. If you don't build it, they are not going to come to you, and you are not going to play.

Another thing that's overlooked. We've focused here on the power of the White House staff to keep the cabinet from the president. My experience was that I was used very frequently by members of the cabinet as the conduit to the president. They wanted to tell the president something but they didn't want to call him, for whatever reason. Maybe they just wanted me to sort of filter the message and say it in a different way. Maybe they just didn't think he needed to be bothered, that it didn't rise to the level of a personal call to the president by a cabinet secretary. So in my experience, the role of a senior White House staff member, from the cabinet's point of view, is frequently that of a communication link to the president, that they choose to use you for.

Presidential appointments. Over time, as the administration proceeded, putting people who we thought politically would serve the president's interest in key senior roles—subsecretary, subcabinet level, key assistant secretary roles and other positions—became an increasing occupier of my time, negotiating with the cabinet secretaries about that.

I remember specifically one of my closest friends on the cabinet, and a person whose appointment to the cabinet at mid-term I was one of the great proponents for, was Moon Landrieu, secretary of HUD, one of the ablest politicians we had on our cabinet.[15] I felt, and the other senior members of the White

---

15. Moon Landrieu was named secretary of the Department of Housing and Urban Development (HUD) on July 27, 1979. He was mayor of New Orleans from 1970 to 1978.

House staff felt, that there was an appointment that needed to be made at a very high level in HUD that we thought was crucial to the president's political interests, and Moon did not want to do that.

And Moon and I—we were good friends—talked, had loggerheads about that, and I finally had to say, because I felt it to be in the president's political interests, "Moon, if you can't do this, then we are going to have to go to the president because here's what I think that needs to be done. We are going to have to take it to the president. Think about it, and if we need to go to the president, let's go." He considered the matter and his decision in that instance was, "Okay, let's don't take it to the president. Let's go with this."

The footnote to that is that it worked out very well, but it was another one of those cases in which a senior White House staffer has to make an effort to be an honest broker, but also to protect the president's interest, to assert the president's interest in dealing with a cabinet member who has, perhaps in that situation, different interests, and try to keep the president out of it.

Arnold Kanter: Was the president aware of this episode while it was unfolding?

Watson: Yes, he was.

Serving the president in terms of negotiating on the budget issues and the legislative issues, trying to reconcile the fights between cabinet members—to come back to Don Rumsfeld's point, which I enthusiastically endorse. By and large, we had, in personal terms, a very compatible cabinet, a very personally compatible, professional group of people.

Berman: Joe Califano?

Watson: Joe Califano, I think, was a strong cabinet member.[16] The problem that we had with Joe—who was and is a friend, who is a man I admire, and who was a good cabinet officer, in my judgment, a good, strong cabinet officer—was that Joe was working all sorts of other agendas on the Hill all the time. (*Laughter*) He had a tendency to say something about tobacco and how it was the weed of the devil when we were trying to make some gain in North Carolina. (*Laughter*)

Joe, of course, was involved and HEW was involved in working out school disputes, quotas in higher education. That was another area in which I constantly got involved with Joe, trying—acting as pure politician, you know, just unmitigatedly looking at the president's political interest, trying to do it in a way that served principle, but motivated by protection of the president's political interest—trying to negotiate with Joe Califano and his immediate subordinates who were working out the deals with North Carolina and Georgia on these school issues and so forth. That was the grist of the day-to-day mill, the grist of talking with them about the presidential appointments, about trying to balance out their disputes with OMB.

---

16. Having served in Johnson's White House as domestic chief of staff, Joseph Califano returned to Democratic service as President Carter's secretary of the Department of Health, Education, and Welfare (HEW) from 1977 until July 1979. Among the reasons Carter offers for Califano's dismissal is that he was "incompatible with the White House staff." Jimmy Carter, *Keeping Faith* (New York: Bantam Books, 1982), p. 116.

Generally speaking, it's my view that cabinet members, the domestic cabinet members with whom I worked most—until I became chief of staff, my responsibilities were really domestic—was that they used the White House staff, Stu Eizenstat [assistant for domestic affairs] and myself principally, as their allies, as their communicators, not always agreeing with them but in dealing with OMB.

Patterson: The grist mill all blew up in the summer of 1979 with an enormous explosion. I don't know about this harmonious cabinet you spoke of.[17]

Watson: When you look at that, there were three cabinet members who left: Brock Adams, Transportation; Schlesinger in Energy, and Blumenthal [at Treasury]. Califano. That's four. That's right, Califano left then. It was Brock Adams who was sort of a delayed departure, but it was all part of the same thing. I'm

---

17. Patterson is referring to a sequence of events that began with Carter's surprise cancellation of a scheduled address to the nation on the energy problem, included a nationally televised address in which Carter characterized the country as gripped in "malaise," and ended with the exodus of three prominent cabinet members and the reorganization of the White House staff under a strong chief of staff. On July 17, 1979, Carter requested the resignations of his entire cabinet, but he then accepted only those of HEW Secretary Joseph Califano, Treasury Secretary Michael Blumenthal, and Energy Secretary James Schlesinger. This episode, interpreted as a disingenuous ploy to remove the three, quickly negated the goodwill generated by Carter's speech. Carter describes the events that led up to the malaise speech and cabinet shuffle in *Keeping Faith*, pp. 114–23. For an example of press treatment of this episode, see Robert Shogan, "Carter Speech, Shakeup Based on Caddell Polls," *Los Angeles Times*, July 25, 1979.

not trying to paint some rosy picture, but if I had to use a phrase, just a catchphrase to summarize the reasons for the departure of Blumenthal, Adams, and Califano—forgive the simplicity—it was because they were not perceived as team players. Whether rightly or wrongly, that's a separate discussion, but the president's perception was that there was not the level and the quality of team participation coming from those three particular cabinet members, all of whom, in their own rights, were formidable people.

Neustadt: I had occasion to talk to Mr. Carter after he was out of office, his views about his staff. Without violating confidences, I think I can probably add two things to what Jack said, and make one of the points I want to emphasize.

One, on Brzezinski. I agree with Jack, as an outside observer, entirely. Mr. Carter doted upon Zbig. He viewed his relationship with Zbig and Zbig and Vance in different terms than the chief of staff did, than I as an outsider did, period. Enough said. Nothing to be done.

Watson: Absolutely.

Neustadt: On Joe Califano. Joe had been a White House staff man at the time. Joe was perfectly controllable, in my judgment, if the president had personally spelled out in no uncertain terms to Joe what he would and wouldn't tolerate. This president wouldn't do that. Nothing to be done. Enough said. The president's always there. Just don't want that forgotten.

Watson: I agree emphatically with both those points.

Rumsfeld: Just several quick points. Dick Neustadt's right that a president's view of the staff is different from a staff's view of the picture. That's not surprising, and it's the combination of the two that begins to give you, I think, a sense of what's going on. No one can live another person's life.

Second, call it professionalism, altruism, desire to see the president succeed for political reasons or desire to see the country do well, people in these jobs end up knowing that the staff system has to have integrity and it is their job to bring that balance and integrity to the job.

Some examples. Jack Watson's absolutely correct, the White House is where all the pressures in society can ultimately come to bear; so there's a great intensity. It's kind of a court of last appeal for people who want something. So the fact that sparks fly up there, I guess, shouldn't surprise us. We are a diverse country and it's inevitable. But one of the tasks of the chief of staff is to see that the president gets views, and presidents have preferences and idiosyncrasies and biases and areas of ignorance, just like all of us do.

Some president may not enjoy a cabinet officer, may not like to be with him. President Ford, I don't think enjoyed Jim Schlesinger, as opposed to respect—totally different. Now, does that mean that the Defense views and Jim Schlesinger's views ought to be cut out of that process? Of course not. They had to be put into the process, and the job of the chief of staff during that period was to assure that, in fact, the Defense input got into the foreign policy and national security decision-making process.

I watched Bob Haldeman with President Nixon,

who was terribly enamored of John Connally, do just the opposite, struggle to get the other views in because the president enjoyed being with John Connally. And Bob—I didn't walk in his shoes, but I was an assistant to President Nixon, a member of the cabinet, a White House official, and I watched it, and I know, just as sure as we are sitting here, that he ran around figuring out ways that Paul McCracken and Herb Stein and George Shultz and all these other people who had input in the economic area, found their way—and Arthur Burns—found their way into these meetings and that their memos found their way to the president.[18] They had to. And that, to me, is the answer to Fred's question about how the staff can help make things better. I'll give you an example of a couple of "saves" that are minor.

President Ford came out of the Congress. Suddenly he's president. He goes up to the Hill. Tip O'Neill puts his arm around him and says, "Come to my birthday party."[19] The president says, "I'll be there." Hell, he's president. He can decide where he wants to go.

He comes back down to the White House. You meet with him five times. He doesn't tell you anything

---

18. John Connally served as President Nixon's secretary of the treasury from early 1971 until May 1972, when he was replaced by George Shultz. Herb Stein and Paul McCracken were members of the Council of Economic Advisors. Arthur Burns served as counselor to the president during the first year of the Nixon administration; from 1970 to 1978 he was chairman of the Federal Reserve System.
19. Thomas P. ("Tip") O'Neill (D-Mass.) entered Congress in 1953. He was majority leader from 1973 to 1976 and became Speaker of the House in 1977.

about it. It's late in the day; he hands you a couple of napkins where he wrote a note or something, and you look at it and he says, "I've agreed to go to Tip O'-Neill's birthday party. It's in seven or eight days." So I come back with a note and I give it to my deputy, Dick Cheney, and Cheney gives it to Jerry Jones or somebody, and they start figuring out where the hell is it and what time is it and who's going to be there and how did they manage that. Turns out one of the Koreans who's under investigation by the Justice Department is paying for the party. (*Laughter*)

So I go back in to the president and I said, "Lookit, I'm not so all fired sure you ought to go to that party."

"What are you talking about, Rummy? Tip's my buddy. I'm going to go to that party." (*Laughter*)

But finally, you know, you work your way out of it and pretty soon, he doesn't go to the party.

Speechwriting. You can have a very good speechwriter who is a very close friend of the president's and has written a couple of spectacular speeches. He begins to believe that the speechwriting process is better if the speech isn't written by a committee, and he's right.

But you've got the fact that the speech is going to say something about something, and you've got all these advisors, the Bill Simons and the Kissingers and the Schlesingers in the world, who are milling around in the substance every day, and you have to take the speech to them so they can look at it and comment on it. Of course, the speechwriter knows that you are going to do that, so the speech comes in late.

Now, what's the chief of staff's job? The chief of

staff has to heave his body in the middle and try to figure out a way for the substantive portions of the speech to finally reach the substantive people so they have a chance to look at it, so the president knows that when he finally gets the speech that, in fact, the substantive people have commented on it.

But what happens when you do that? That's throwing sand in the gears and it gets grindy, and pretty soon, out come news stories that Cheney is having a fight with the speechwriter or something. He *isn't* having a fight with the speechwriter. He couldn't care less about the speechwriter. All he wants is for the ultimate product to accomplish what the president intended. It isn't personal. It is not personal at all, and yet that's where the rubber hits the ground. And if there's no rubber on the tire, it's steel, and that's sparks.

Cheney: To follow up and close the loop on Don's comments on the Ford administration and come back around to politics and to Dave Broder's question about the vice-presidency: there's another function in there, in addition to trying to help do something positive, which is to be the cushion that takes the pain and the heat, oftentimes not only externally but also internally.

In the Ford administration, we had major problems in managing the vice-presidential relationship. I think the Carter administration and Reagan administration subsequently have done much better. But President Ford came in and, because he'd been vice-president, wanted to have substantive responsibility assigned to the vice-president. He picked Nelson

Rockefeller because he was the kind of man of stature that he needed as an unelected president in his own right.

As Don made some reference to yesterday, President Ford put the vice-president in charge of all domestic policy making, put him in charge of the Domestic Council, gave him the assignment of creating new policy, and let him staff the operation out. Everybody on the staff said, "Mr. President, you shouldn't do that. It's going to create conflict." But the president is the president. He went ahead and made the decision to do it anyway. But repeatedly after that, at his regular Wednesday afternoon meetings, the vice-president would come in with a new policy proposal for the president, new health insurance scheme or new economic policy initiative of some kind. He'd lay it on the president, and the president would take it.

At the end of the day, you'd go down for the final close-out session, and the president would hand it to you and say, "What the hell do we do with this?" Your responsibility at that point was to say, "Well, we'll staff it out," and then take it and send it out through the system. The answer would always come back—it never failed—it always came back exactly the same way, "This new policy proposal is totally inconsistent with the basic policy of the Ford administration."

So in effect then, you'd end up having been, as Don said, the sand in the gears. An initiative that might have made all the sense in the world to Nelson Rockefeller was shot down. From the standpoint of the vice-president, you are a bad guy, an obstacle to his opportunity to have a significant impact on policy.

The ultimate result is great personal hostility between, in my case, myself and the vice-president, and Don before that.

About this time, Nelson Rockefeller became the first vice-president to have the new vice-presidential quarters in Washington. The chief of naval operations' quarters had been turned over to the vice-president as his official residence, and after he got it all decorated and everything, he never lived in it because he had a nicer house up on Foxhall Road. (*Laughter*)

But he had a series of parties to break in the house. He invited everybody in the press corps, everybody in the administration, everybody on Capitol Hill in a series of events to visit the vice-president's house. I was never in the vice-president's house until Walter Mondale was vice-president, and I was the only individual in town who was never invited to one of those affairs. It was unfortunate, it was difficult, but from the standpoint of the president, it was absolutely essential. He ended up having a good relationship with Nelson Rockefeller.

But I was the SOB, and on a number of occasions, got involved in shouting matches with the vice-president. He finally told Ford at one point that the only way he would serve in a second Ford administration as vice-president was if he could also be chief of staff. If you ask President Ford today why that relationship was strained, it was always the staff problem with the vice-president. His relationship with the vice-president was excellent.

But the problem, in fact, was created by the pres-

ident. We had to deal with it, and the staff's responsibility in this case was to be that cushion, that rubber, basically, between the president and vice-
president. It made their relationship sound, kept us
from doing anything that was stupid in terms of
administration policy overall, but made you the
brunt of great hostility from one of the senior people
in the administration.

Goodpaster: I think that in our administration such personality issues were not only secondary, they were
way secondary. The primary issue was the setting of
the policy, the setting of the political direction, and
the taking of specific and often very hard political decisions. And on that, thanks to what Don called the
de Staercke precept, the skin was such that you
didn't see the digestive process.

I'll pick out a couple of examples on the economic
side. That's vitally important to the political direction. The president and some of his principal people
had the clear vision, but there were conflicting views,
for example, between the secretary of the treasury
and the chairman of the Council of Economic Advisors, and these were carried to the point of harsh confrontation. Didn't become public.

But I recall that Governor Adams had the task of
seeing what could be done to define the issue and
what could be done to resolve it. Time was marching
on, the economic message had to be sent up to the
Congress, and here was something that had to be resolved. And Adams, in his careful and thoughtful and
firm way, had this discussed between the people involved, found out what the issue was, and was able

finally to work it out in a way that they then took to the president, and that satisfied the requirement.

In trade policy, too, we had sharp disagreement, and again, you'd have a cabinet officer saying, "That's not what we came down here to do," and real confrontation that needed to be resolved. In this case, Gabe Hauge, who was assistant to the president with responsibility in the economic area, had the people in from Commerce, from State, others that were interested in it, and gradually was able to bring out a position which then had to be taken up to the Hill. And you had confrontation there with senior legislative leaders of the president's own party who were quite adamantly opposed to move in the direction of freer trade. That had to be worked out.

Adams and General Persons, who headed up the legislative liaison, had the people down, sorted out the differences, finally came to a view in this area. The president established a special assistant, Clarence Randall, who would work in the area of trade policy to try to build consensus which could then obtain the agreement up on the Hill.[20]

But because the focus of the president was on what he regarded as the primary aspect of the decision and the policy and because he had no time for any indulgence in personality issues, people would have been ashamed to take that to him, and he would have

---

20. After Sherman Adams resigned as White House chief of staff in 1958, Major General Wilton B. Persons served in that capacity until the end of Eisenhower's term. Clarence Randall was special consultant to the president and later special assistant to the president.

made them ashamed. "Is this your idea of how to serve the country?" They didn't want to hear him ask that kind of a question, and so we were able to get resolution there.

Rumsfeld: A lot depends on how good a manager the president is. How much turmoil goes down below and ends up disrupting things depends on how skillful a manager he is. I'll give you an example.

President, East Wing, sends down the list for the state dinner for Helmut Schmidt, the West German chancellor. Cabinet officer is not on it. There's only so many slots for a state dinner. The cabinet officer comes to the chief of staff and says, "I've got to be at that dinner. I'm secretary of *X*. I deal with them all the time on this. It will look like I'm downgraded." And the chief of staff says, "You've got a point. Let me see what I can do."

You go in to the president and say, "Look, this guy needs it to do his job effectively, to be on it." He says, "Look, Betty just came up with this list. The guy's been at the last four straight. I've got a couple of political guys I want to add in there. There's a limit. No." And I say, "Fine. Just keep it in the back of your mind. Someone will cancel and we'll jam him in." You go out of the office. Three days later, the cabinet officer's in there and says, "Oh, by the way, Mr. President, I'm not on the list." The president says, "You're kidding. Let me see what I can do." (*Laughter*)

Haldeman: Somebody screwed up again.

Rumsfeld: The president wants everyone to like him. So that night, last thing you know, it comes on a napkin and he's got a little note, "Let's put that fellow back on."

What does that guy think? He is convinced that you tried to cut him out.

Popkin: He thinks you never told the president.

Rumsfeld: Exactly. Or that you had some scheme or something, and who could care less who goes to the lousy dinner?

Goodpaster: Those are areas where resolution was accomplished. Occasionally you come to an impasse, and you come to an impasse between the administration, we will say, between the executive branch and the Congress, and here, the president and his staff simply are unable to achieve agreement. Then you have to resort to the raw powers of the president, for example, to keep a Bricker amendment from passing.[21] A lot of damage gets strewn up around the Hill because in the president's own party, there is a commitment to forcing that amendment through the Congress.

There's another way of dealing with these things. Again, concessions have to be made. You may have stress between your attorney general, we will say, and the leading figures on the Hill whose support the president absolutely requires over an issue in the social area, such as racial relations, the extension of desegregation. Ultimately, you have a Little Rock, a crisis that perhaps could and should have been headed

---

21. On the Bricker amendment, see note 34 to the first session.

off by dealing with it in some more effective way earlier.[22] Not a matter of personalities, but a very deep clash of convictions, a real test of the president. Ultimately it comes to him. The chief of staff, as Don says, takes the heat on many of these, but some of them simply cannot be resolved short of the president himself, and some of them, he can't resolve. But that's the test of the president, I would say.

Sorensen: Since we've spent two days here largely exercising self-glorification, let me offer two less dramatic but, I think, highly illustrative examples of the advantages of ignorance; in this case, my ignorance.

We had a sharp division of opinion in the Kennedy administration between the State and Treasury regarding the international balance of payments. It wasn't a personality issue, but let's not kid ourselves that policy issues, if allowed to fester, become personality issues. It was largely at the under-secretary level. The president, knowing very, very little about

---

22. In an effort to block the planned integration of Little Rock's Central High School in September 1957, Governor Orval E. Faubus ordered the Arkansas National Guard to prevent nine black students from entering the school. On September 14, Faubus met with Eisenhower, but no agreement to desegregate the school was reached. On September 24, Eisenhower federalized the Arkansas Guard in order to remove them from the governor's command, and he sent five hundred soldiers from the 101st Airborne to ensure the safe passage of the black students into the school. These events are recounted by Emmet John Hughes in *The Ordeal of Power: A Political Memoir of the Eisenhower Years* (New York: Atheneum, 1963) pp. 241–45. Richard E. Neustadt offers this episode as an instructive instance of the political costs that attend presidential command; see his *Presidential Power*, rev. ed. (New York: Wiley, 1980), pp. 10–23.

international monetary policy, turned to the only person in the administration who knew even less, me, and said, "Well, you work this out." (*Laughter*)

Kernell: Is this the task-force approach we have heard so much about?

Sorensen: I began a series of meetings in my office between the under secretary of state, George Ball, and the under secretary of the treasury, Bob Roosa. At times in the beginning, they were a little acrimonious, but they both trusted me completely because they knew I knew absolutely nothing about it. Therefore, I had an open mind. I'd doze a little sometimes while they were arguing, and I asked the dumbest questions imaginable. And by that process, sooner or later, a program emerged, a policy emerged, and they were harmonious thereafter.

My second undramatic example was not a policy battle or a personality battle, but a turf battle, and those are the most fierce in Washington. The secretary of interior, Stewart Udall, came to see me. I can't remember what the issue was, but it was a battle over jurisdiction of some kind with the chairman of the Federal Power Commission, Joe Swidler. Well, I didn't know what the decision would be. I didn't know who was in the right and so on. But Udall said Swidler wouldn't talk to him because Swidler said he was the chairman of an independent agency, and all the political science books say that independent agencies don't have to kowtow to executive management. I said, "Well, that's unfortunate." (*Laughter*)

I did nothing whatsoever. After a period of time passed, Joe Swidler called me and he said, "Gee, my request for a budget for next year has been sitting on your desk for a very long time. What's happened? I've got to make some plans." I said, "Gee, Joe, I've got a stack of them on my desk. Yours unfortunately is at the bottom of the pile. I've got so many other things I'm trying to work out. For example, that problem between you and Udall. I don't know what to do about that, but I sure wish you'd talk to him about it. If I get that off my desk, I might have time to get back to the pile." (*Laughter*)

He said, "Well, no, no, that's a question of the rights of an independent agency."

"Okay. Well, I'm sure it is."

He called me back ten days later and said, "What about that budget request?" And I said, "Gee, Joe, yours is still at the bottom of the pile." Next day, he saw Udall, and the matter was resolved.

Watson: Let me add just one quick one. People have different images. We have got the Rumsfeld image of the White House chief of staff as the grease, or the sand, on occasion. A friend of mine asked me if the White House chief of staff was more like, in sports terms, a quarterback, which is sort of the glorified image, or a goalie or a utility infielder.

Kernell: Or a cheerleader.

Watson: Or a cheerleader. I said the image that comes to my mind, borne out by some of the stories being told this morning, is that of javelin catcher. (*Laughter*)

Haldeman: Excellent.

Rumsfeld: One thing we haven't even talked about is turbulence in government, the fact that so many of these

people hold these jobs for such short terms. If I ran
G. D. Searle the way the government of the United
States is run, it would go broke in five minutes. You
have had four national security advisors in the Reagan administration in five years. That is not healthy
for this country.

It is damaging, and it is something that we ought
to think about. You don't get good at those jobs in five
minutes, and if there's anything we know, it's people
get out on that track and fall into the same damn pot-
holes that their predecessors fell in. With a job as important as that, it seems to me that it's important
that there be some stability; the same is true for some
of the other key jobs. There are other jobs, though,
that you can change every five minutes, and the
world would go on just fine.

Transition periods

Kernell: That raises another issue that we haven't talked
about yet. A president comes in and typically has to
make something like three thousand appointments.
How do you make those appointments? Where do the
names come from? Coming out of the campaign, how
do you set up an organization to govern?

Bob, could you begin with a discussion of that?

Haldeman: Yes. I wish Harry McPherson were here because we had, I think, an ideal transition, as ideal as
a transition can be from one party to the other, from

the Johnson administration to the Nixon administration, primarily because President Johnson ordered his administration to make it the ideal transition of all time, the standard for how transitions
should be conducted. All of his cabinet officers, all of
his staff people cooperated with all of our counterparts as the process went on. That part worked extremely well.

The thing that I would hope that our discussion
here might yield is an understanding of the complexity of this job of the White House staff operation and
of the conduct of the office of the presidency. We have
come up with a lot of similarities between the various
operations that we've all had, despite the different
parties and vastly different characters and characteristics of our presidents. You've got to also recognize that there are enormous differences and that
maybe we haven't really spelled those out adequately.

Regarding the transition period, you've got to remember that the executive branch of the United
States is, I think, the largest corporation in the world.
It has the most awesome responsibilities of any corporation in the world, the largest budget of any corporation in the world, and the largest number of employees of any corporation in the world. Yet the entire
senior-management structure and team of that corporation has to be formed in a period of seventy-five
days, give or take a day or two, from election day in
November until inauguration day in January. The executive office has to be formed from absolute zero
into a structure and an organization that is running
full steam with total responsibility as of 12:00 noon

on January 20 for every aspect of its operation. No way to look back. Every order that the previous president has issued may continue being carried out, but you are responsible for it now if you don't rescind it.

You've got to find the people to staff that senior management of the corporation. You've got to qualify them, put them in place, train them, and coordinate them. You've got to set up the White House staff, the president's staff, based partly on people that he knows, trusts, and has dealt with, partly on people that he doesn't know and hasn't dealt with, because there aren't enough people within his own purview to properly staff it.

You have to bring in people with vast experience in government and you have to bring in some people with no experience in government but with experience in other areas that will relate to what's being done. That point was raised in one of the earlier discussions by Dick Neustadt: staff with previous government experience versus those with no experience. I am one of those two, I guess, at the table who had no previous government experience.

If all of us in our administration had had no previous government experience, and most importantly, if our president had had no previous government experience, which some presidents have not had, that would have been disastrous. But President Nixon did have enormous experience in government at the legislative and executive level, and he had an intimate personal working rapport with the vast number of people who themselves had enormous experience in government. So the fact that I did or didn't have government experience was not a vital factor. Under other circumstances, it could or would have been an issue.

I had had management experience, but more importantly I had had an extremely strong and intimate working relationship with the president himself. That's the absolute vital factor in the chief of staff's role.

Structuring the staff with the kind and range of people you need to be ready to roll on January 20 is an awesome enterprise to have to undertake. It occurs to you rather quickly on election night, right after the final announcement is made that you've won, you figure, "Now, we can take a vacation." But then you realize that the vacation is going to be four or eight years from now.

I think it is important for anyone who deals with the White House staff to realize that it is not built, as most corporations are, over many years, with people training, working their way up into various positions, getting lots of experience. The White House has to put its staff together instantly. It's the ultimate fast-food operation and it's got to produce great hamburgers on the first round off the skillet.

You don't have much time for trial-and-error, and maybe that explains some of the personal differences within a group. You've put a totally disparate group together and said, "You guys all work together." That, it seems to me, is the importance of the skin that Rummy talks about. You've got to give us a chance to run that digestive process without your picking up the skin all the time and looking under to see how it's going. It's like planting seeds and then digging them up to see if the flower is coming up. You have to let your seeds grow. Let a staff come together, give it that honeymoon which, in all fairness, the press does seem to do. There does seem to be some understanding of that in the early days of an administration.

But as the differences and problems arise, they have to be worked out internally. The administration has to have some leeway within its house to get those problems resolved before we have to step out on the front porch and tell you that we are having a problem. The way that's done is with a strong staff organization, with a strong understanding within that staff organization as to the roles of the staff and their responsibilities to the president, with a strong loyalty to the president and commitment to the president, and a recognition that they serve him first and, through him, the country, because the executive branch under the Constitution is only one guy, the president of the United States.

The move to build a team and deal with problems that occur can be handled internally if it doesn't have to be aired every second on the second, at least. It can be dealt with much more effectively without creating additional problems if there is that opportunity and that understanding. That means a strong staff.

Despite the desire to possibly be able to build a structure that doesn't require a coordinator, I personally don't believe that's possible and I'm not even really convinced it's desirable. Someone has to be the person to whom the others know they can turn and can trust.

The value of ignorance, as Ted pointed out, is enormous. I had, and had no problem proving it, a total ignorance as to the operation of the executive branch of the government. I was therefore accepted by those with experience and those without as an honest broker, and I dealt with them that way because I knew my entire existence with those people depended upon their acceptance of me as an honest broker. After some trial-and-error and some very adroit attempts at end-runs by the shrewd politicians, they came to realize that they could best get things done by dealing through the system that was set up. It was set up to accomplish something that it *was* accomplishing, and most of them, most of the time, relied on it.

Each of them at some time didn't, and that's understandable, expectable, and we were set up to deal with that, too. We expected end-runs, and we wanted them to end-run. There are times when it's essential that the chief of staff be end-runned. Every senior staff person, every cabinet officer in our administration—and I'm sure it's true in all the rest of them—knew that if he really had to and really wanted to, he could get to the president and he could say what he needed to say to the president. Most of them didn't do it, as Andy says, because they didn't want to hear what the president would say in response to an end-run.

Kernell: There are two other staff people here who served during transition periods. Jack or Ted, are there things that Bob said that you would like to respond to or endorse?

Watson: All our problems in the transition of 1976 were self-imposed problems. They were problems on our incoming side, problems of integrating campaign staff with transition planners, problems between reconciliation of those disparate groups with disparate interests, to some extent, with Hamilton Jordan and myself. Someone said that "It was two months into the transition before I felt safe in starting my own car." (*Laughter*)

But I will say, and I believe this is true, that I cannot imagine having had a more forthcoming, candid, open-handed cooperation from Dick Cheney and from Don Rumsfeld and from Jack Marsh than we had. I don't think they withheld any effort to help our transition, and I've always been really grateful for that.

Sorensen: The most important decision the president has to make in the transition period, more important than deciding what his policy or his state of the union message will be or even his secretary of state, is his choice of his principal White House staff. Why is it that the eight men who participated around this table in these two days, men of such disparate views and political philosophies, have had such agreement and harmony? I think it's because, if I may say so immodestly, we are all professionals with a dedication to effective U.S. government.

All our presidents selected for various positions cronies or political hangers-on or whatever, but every president knows when he's picking his chief of staff, my god, he'd better get the right man in that job or he'll be ruined. Every president picks very carefully the person who he believes can fulfill that function. I'll just close by noting that the present White House chief of staff was picked for Reagan, in effect, and it remains to be seen how that works out.

Closing remarks

Popkin: In closing, I'm going to ask Jerry Warren to say a few words, as the man who put this together.

Gerald Warren: Thank you, Sam. I feel like the junior leaguer who would not go to the orgy because she didn't want to write all those thank-you letters. (*Laughter*)

I hope that this discussion has shown these gentlemen to be, as Ted says, thorough professionals who want to do the best for the U.S. government because, regardless of their total dedication to one man, when they walk into that White House, when they sit down in the first week of their duties, they realize that they are not just protectors and servers of the president, but of the institution, the office of the presidency. That's why the institution is so strong, and that's why, as Ted pointed out yesterday, it has survived.

I hope something else comes out of this, too. That the American press understands that when Bob Hartmann leaks to Evans and Novak that Haig is keeping all those Nixon folks in the White House, he's doing that because he doesn't want to attack Jerry Ford.[23] It's Jerry Ford who's doing it, not Al Haig. It was

---

23. Robert Hartmann served as Gerald Ford's chief assistant in Congress, then moved with him when Ford assumed the vice-presidency, and later served as a speechwriter in the Ford White House. Reflecting perhaps his reduced status within the larger staff, Hartmann later wrote an unflattering portrait of some of his colleagues: *Palace Politics: An Insider's Account of the Ford Years* (New York: McGraw-Hill, 1980).

Richard Nixon who didn't want to see the transportation secretary, not Bob Haldeman.

Remember that wonderful White House worship service?

Haldeman: Yes.

Warren: [Volpe] had not been able to see the president for so long that he walked up in the receiving line after the worship service, shook the president's hand, took a three-by-five card out of his pocket, and began going down his agenda.[24] (*Laughter*)

I do want to pay particular tribute to Peter Kaye, who is going to be producing the TV show for PBS.

John Chancellor, you were just wonderful. Is there anything you want to say to close this orgy?

Chancellor: I had fun. I think we all did.

---

24. John Volpe served as secretary of the Department of Transportation from January 1969 to January 1973.

THE CREED AND REALITY
OF MODERN WHITE HOUSE
MANAGEMENT

The foregoing discussions offer us a puzzle of some consequence. How is it that these eight men—who entered presidential service from such diverse backgrounds and who in office served presidents with distinctly different political goals and work habits—should find themselves agreeing on the essentials of modern White House management? And how is it that these former senior aides, rather than offer a rationale to account for the modern White House staff's expanded mandate and growth, espouse the professional creed first articulated nearly half a century ago, when the presidential staffing system was quite different from the one used today? The creed enunciated in these sessions is familiar stuff to students of the institutional history of the presidency: The president's aides should have a passion for anonymity; when it comes to the size of the White House staff, small is beau-

The author wishes to thank Terry Moe, Sam Popkin, and Larry Rothenberg for their helpful comments on an earlier version of this essay.

193

tiful; and the primary duty of a senior aide is to coordinate the flow of information to and from the Oval Office. But one is surprised to hear these views voiced by Haldeman, Haig, and the other aides who presided over the steady expansion of the staff's mandate and power. More than lip service is being offered here, as the panelists speak with convincing sincerity, at times with revealing candor, and consistently illustrate their views with persuasive anecdotes. How is it that these former chiefs, all sounding like Louis Brownlow's disciples, embrace a creed that political observers charge has long been abandoned by White House staffs?

More than idle curiosity is at stake. The persistence of the venerable creed, despite the substantial changes that have reworked the White House office during the post–World War II era, makes for a more complex organization than has generally been depicted. The durability of the creed is also a sign of continuity in an institution that is necessarily reconstituted with each new administration. By understanding why the normative order persists, how modern aides reconcile it with their daily duties, and how over time it has directed and restrained the White House's evolution, we shall gain a new appreciation of the president's staff as an institution.

The Apparent Discrepancy of Creed and Reality

The panelists' invocations of Brownlow at first seem at odds with the public behavior of recent senior presidential aides. Few observers would describe White House senior staff as adhering strictly to the Brownlow committee's dictum to "remain in the background, issue no orders, make no decisions, emit no public statements."[1] Let us begin by surveying how well the assertions of fidelity to Brownlow's creed stack up against the realities of the job, at least as they appear to outsiders.

The "passion for anonymity"

H. R. Haldeman, who because of Watergate remains among the most well-known former chiefs, lets us know early on that we are in for surprises when he emphatically endorses Brownlow's "passion for anonymity" as a vital virtue for staff: "I completely agree with the Brownlow plan, that the White House staff should be an operational unit, not a policy-making or policy-executing unit. It should be there to assist the president in the management of the executive branch and in the office of the president." Toward this end "virtually all the staff members," Haldeman insists, must be "people with Brownlow's passion for anonymity." When Chancellor canvasses the participants about their public appearances, none reports having ventured more than once or twice onto a network public affairs program.

Desiring anonymity and having it are the difference between ambition and success. Events inevitably make those close to the president newsworthy, and a strong

---

1. Herbert Emmerich, *Federal Organization and Administrative Management* (University: University of Alabama Press, 1971), p. 54.

chief of staff like Haldeman will attract news despite his best efforts to remain out of the public limelight. When Brownlow first used the phrase "passion for anonymity" during a briefing, Franklin Roosevelt laughed and exclaimed that whoever came up with that idea "doesn't know his American press."[2]

But the visibility, even notoriety, of senior staff today appears to be fueled by more than the natural desire of the press to report on the foibles of people in power. One contributing factor is that presidential aides conduct so much of their business in public, a tendency exemplified by recent controversies involving President Reagan's past and present aides. In early March 1986, for example, the administration lost a close budget vote in the House of Representatives. When asked to explain the president's defeat, Republican House leaders carped that Chief of Staff Donald Regan had acted as though Congress were his board of directors and he the government's "chief executive officer"—which is precisely how Regan had recently described his job to a reporter.[3] Less than a month later President Reagan lost another close vote in the House, this time on military aid to the Contra forces in Nicaragua. Many Democrats claimed they had been disposed to support the legislation until White House Director of Communications Patrick Buchanan launched a public campaign besmirching congressional opponents with charges of abetting communist expansion. Perhaps Buchanan is correct in arguing that he merely provided

---

2. Cited in Louis Brownlow, *The Passion for Anonymity* (Chicago: University of Chicago Press, 1958), 2: 381.
3. Bernard Weinraub, "How Donald Regan Runs the White House," *New York Times Magazine*, January 5, 1986.

these congressmen with a convenient foil, which enabled them to oppose the military aid program without picking a fight with a popular president.[4] The fact, however, that an aide had gained sufficient visibility to make him a suitable target distinguishes the contemporary staff from its predecessors.

The theme of the Buchanan squabble recalls for Washington observers the widely publicized and controversial reassignment of Health and Human Services Secretary Margaret Heckler as ambassador to Ireland. She resisted, publicly charging that she was being sacked by Chief of Staff Regan for failing to be a "team player"—another instance of an antagonist attacking the president's aide to skirt a costly fight with the president. Eventually, Heckler succumbed to the call to diplomatic service, but not before Washington correspondents had filed numerous stories reporting gossip from anonymous White House sources and expressions of sympathy from her friends on Capitol Hill.

In late April 1986 two of Reagan's former aides returned to the Washington limelight in ways that added to the administration's embarrassment. With great fanfare former budget director David Stockman held a series of well-staged press conferences and television interviews to promote his "tell-all" book, for which he had earned a $2 million advance. Michael Deaver, a member of the "troika" that ran the White House during Reagan's first term, should have had more modest aspirations for

---

4. Robert W. Merry, "Reagan's Risky Tack Ties Defeat of Contra Aid to Soviet Takeover or U.S. Invasion of Nicaragua," *Wall Street Journal*, March 5, 1986; Sara Fritz, "Contras Lobby Angers Swing-Vote Democrats," *Los Angeles Times*, March 19, 1986.

publicity when he returned as a lobbyist representing the interests of his new clients to his former associates in the administration. Unfortunately, the need for discretion escaped him. An early March 1986 issue of *Time* had on its cover a posed photo of Deaver making the lobbying rounds in his limousine. As conflict-of-interest charges mounted in Congress and the press, Deaver garnered the Reagan White House more adverse publicity than had Stockman. Recent events have thus borne out Bob Haldeman's comparison of senior White House aides with movie stars.

As the modern White House has accumulated the resources and mandate necessary to make it a key player in Washington's institutional politics, the job of the senior assistant has been transformed. The anonymous go-between of yesteryear is sometimes today asked to be a "point man," or as in the case of Haldeman's single television appearance, a provocateur. The discreet aide steeped in neutral competence and honest brokerage has (necessarily) been succeeded by celebrity politicians who actively pursue the president's policy goals with other politicians in the executive branch and beyond.

Small is beautiful

Criticism of the White House staff has intensified as its numbers have swollen. With so many members of President Nixon's White House implicated in one or more of the misdeeds lumped under the rubric of Watergate, staff growth became an issue of some urgency. In his campaign debates with President Ford, Jimmy Carter tried to focus the electorate's attention on staff size. It is not too surprising, then, that these former chiefs who presided over the steady growth of the White House would be put on the spot. What is surprising is that rather than defend growth with a recitation of the "burdens of the office," they describe it as an unfortunate development that somehow must be dealt with. Sorensen, who served in a White House that was sparse by current standards, cautions, "If you have hundreds of people [invoking the president's name], there is no way you can keep them out of mischief." Rumsfeld avers, "There's a natural tendency for staff to grow," a tendency that must be countered, he suggests, by moving more issues out to the departments. Haig, who worked in the largest White House to date, is the most emphatic of all. He calls the growth in staff "horrendous" and adds, "The leaner and meaner you are, the more effective your White House will be."

Against this collective consternation, we need to weigh in the historical record of what took place in the White House organization during these aides' watch. As reflected in these discussions, estimates of staff size vary depending upon how deeply one delves into the organization. If one includes security and custodial employees, staffers number in the thousands. Under the most restrictive definition, limiting "staff" to professional aides, high-level Civil Service–grade appointments, and executive-level positions in the White House, the size of the staff drops to under a hundred.[5] The most commonly

---

5. Using budget figures and information from the OMB, Richard E. Neustadt estimated the numbers of "civilian aides with some substantive part in public business": 22 in 1952; over 30 in the mid-1950s; 22 in 1962; between 50 and 75 in 1972. Neustadt, "The Constraining of the President," *New York Times Magazine*, October 14, 1973. In comparison, Emmerich estimates that the White House office contained about 100 professionals in 1969 (*Federal Organization*, p. 242).

cited estimates, however, follow the annual budget in defining "staff" as all professional and clerical workers in the White House office. Even these figures are suspect, though, because presidents, well before Franklin Roosevelt, have "detailed" additional staff from various departments. More accurate estimates are available thanks to archival research commissioned by the House Committee on Post Office and Civil Service in the early 1970s and to a rule enacted in 1979 that requires the president to identify annually the number of detailees working in the White House. These data (see Figure 1) portray the relatively uninterrupted growth of the White House staff from 1939 until 1975, when, in reaction to Watergate, the staff began to shrink.[6]

Having long ago surpassed the charmed size of a group governed by personal relations, the White House office today can be fairly labeled a bureaucracy. The entourage of presidential confidants envisioned by Brownlow has rapidly evolved into a multifunctional firm, replete with diversification of tasks and the recruitment of experts into specialized roles. This difference is well illustrated by the contrast between the organizational structure of the Reagan White House (Figure 2) and President Roosevelt's insistence that any reform proposals not confine his staff to organizational "boxes."

The increases in the size and visibility of the White

---

6. The post-Watergate figures can be deceptive, however, since Jimmy Carter transferred some positions out of the White House office proper to other units of the executive office. Fred I. Greenstein, "Nine Presidents in Search of a Modern Presidency," in Anthony King (ed.), *The New American Political System*, 2d ed. (Washington, D.C.: American Enterprise Institute, forthcoming).

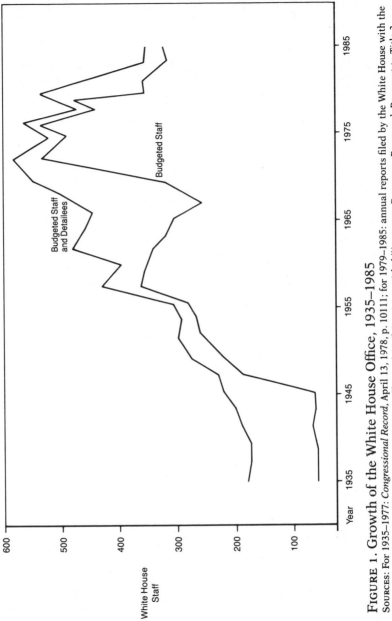

FIGURE 1. Growth of the White House Office, 1935–1985

SOURCES: For 1935–1977: *Congressional Record*, April 13, 1978, p. 10111; for 1979–1985: annual reports filed by the White House with the House of Representatives Committee on Post Office and Civil Service, entitled "Aggregate Report on Personnel, Pursuant to Title 3, United States Code, Section 113"; and *Budget of the United States Government*. NOTE: Number of detailees for 1981 unavailable.

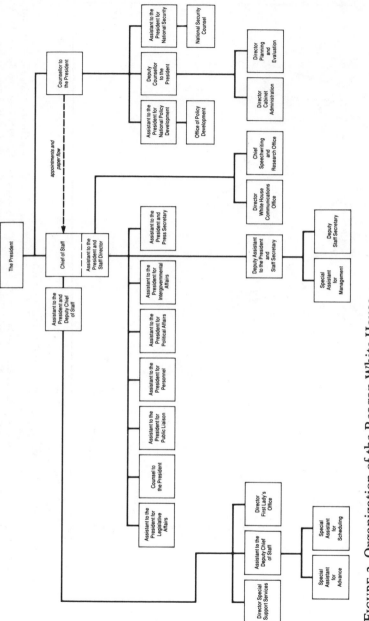

FIGURE 2. Organization of the Reagan White House

SOURCE: John Kessel, *Presidency Research Group Newsletter* 3, no. 2 (April 1981). Kessel received the information from James Baker, then White House chief of staff.

House staff reflect the ever-expanding mandate presidents bestow on their aides. Tasks that used to be performed in the departments and party organizations compose a substantial share of the routine work of the modern White House. This expanding repertoire of roles has been accompanied by structures for the specialized division of labor. Personnel are frequently recruited into the White House according to their expertise, and presidential aides are expected to originate policies and supervise the activities of staff in the departments and executive agencies. More than a decade ago, Thomas E. Cronin summed up the presidential scholars' concern with these developments: "The Presidency has become a large bureaucracy itself, rapidly acquiring many dubious characteristics of large bureaucracies in the process: layering, overspecialization, communication gaps, inadequate coordination and an impulse to become consumed with short-term operational concerns."[7]

Coordination versus management

It is on the subject of the senior aide as a coordinator, or in Jack Watson's words, an "honest broker," that the chiefs give the most eloquent expression to traditional values. In order to distinguish the class of administrative duties Brownlow and his associates intended for staff from those they wished to reserve for the president, we need to define *coordination* and *management* more pre-

---

7. Thomas E. Cronin, "The Swelling of the Presidency," *The Saturday Review of the Society*, February 1973.

cisely than general usage does. In the lexicon of administrative science, which guided these architects of the institutional presidency, these terms connote quite different aspects of administration. It is the same difference, critics charge, that distinguishes the creed from the reality of presidential staff behavior today.

Above all, the members of the Brownlow committee sought to construct a strong foundation on which the president could assume control of the executive branch. In large part this entailed expanding his manpower base; but a prior issue had to be resolved. Neither the Constitution nor political practice gave the president sufficient authority to assume day-to-day responsibility for running the government. What was needed, the committee knew, was a rationale that legitimized and delineated the boundaries of the president's routine involvement in the affairs of the executive departments. Just such a rationale was offered by the burgeoning field of scientific management: The federal government could be modeled on the modern corporation.[8] Just like a corporation, the government required a chief executive officer, a manager who would ensure that the individual "line" agencies functioned coherently and responsively. The chief executive officer of the government was, of course, the president.

---

8. In a historic meeting at the White House with the leaders of Congress, Roosevelt unveiled the Brownlow committee's proposals and sounded the theme of the managerial presidency: "I like the word 'management.' It is popular and this thing [reform proposal] is going to be popular. People talk of a good housewife as a 'good manager' and when the father of a big family runs things well he is called a 'good manager.' The problem of better administrative management is one that has troubled me for some time." Emmerich, *Federal Organization*, p. 207.

The corporate analogy not only legitimized presidential involvement in the executive departments, it identified the kinds of resources a president qua manager required. Since fiscal, planning, and personnel decisions composed the primary "staff" functions of corporate managers, Brownlow's committee called for the creation of the Executive Office of the President and the relocation there of the Bureau of the Budget (then housed in the Department of the Treasury), the National Resources Board, and the independent Civil Service Commission.

Since the executive departments were to report to the White House and to respond to its direction, the committee proposed that the White House office include a small number of aides who would routinely check on these line activities and report back to the president. Although other arrangements to fill in the interstices between the president and the departments were deducible from scientific management theory, this was the system Roosevelt wanted, and the committee members happily complied. In this way, *management* came to refer to those activities by which the president administered the government.

Coordination, by comparison, remains even today a more loosely defined concept in administrative science. For the president's staff, *coordination* involves such activities as providing the president with information, relaying messages to those in the line agencies, maintaining the president's calendar, giving him technical advice when he solicits it, and generally performing whatever duties a manager could reasonably ask of a factotum.[9] As

9. President Roosevelt often cited his need for legal counsel on legislation and policies, advice that was sometimes difficult to obtain from the "overburdened" Justice Department.

aides *coordinate* the movement of men and messages to and from the Oval Office, they help the president *manage* the government. Yet presidents must *coordinate* the activities of their staffs in order to *manage* the activities of those beyond. Giving out assignments, delegating authority to oversee particular projects, and refereeing disputes among deputies are among the housekeeping duties that must be performed if the White House is to work smoothly.

While presidential coordination is a lesser matter, it is by no means trivial. In his memoirs, Brownlow describes the circumstances that first attracted Roosevelt to the notion of appointing an outside committee to study administrative reform. In 1935 Congress gave the president $4.8 billion to set up an assortment of relief programs. In what soon came to be known as the "five-ring circus," Roosevelt created new agencies close to the White House and headed for the most part by his closest aides. The president served on the governing committees of these agencies and, by one account, his attendance was frequently required to snuff out smoldering conflicts among aides. The cumulative result, in Brownlow's words, was that the president himself shouldered "the tremendous burden of the actual task of coordination." Exhausted and frustrated by having to do it all himself, Roosevelt confided to Brownlow that "something ought to be done to give the President more effective control over the general management of the government."[10] Roosevelt never relinquished responsibility for coordinating the activities of his staff, but by 1935 even he be-

---

10. Brownlow, *Passion for Anonymity*, 2:325.

gan to feel overwhelmed by the volume of business flowing into the Oval Office.

In Brownlow's schema, the difference between a
manager and a coordinator is identical to that between
a president and his staff. Unquestionably, modern presidents expect their senior aides to assume more responsibility for management than envisioned by Brownlow,
yet the panelists come down squarely in favor of the more
confined role of coordination. The most assertive actions
they admit to having taken are having run interference
for the president and having engaged occasionally in benign subterfuge to protect him from his own ill-consid-
ered opinions. Alexander Haig volunteers, "This tendency for the White House staff to put themselves in a
position where they determine policy and act in behalf of
the president across the full range of our policy [is a] very
dangerous, pernicious reality." Instead of tales of ag-
gressive management characterized by conflict and confrontation, these chiefs offer less venturesome stories of
working mostly as professional coordinators. Almost dis-
interestedly, they broker policy disagreements among
departments, solicit opposing points of view for the president's consideration, assuage the ire of a cabinet member who feels slighted by a colleague or perhaps by the
president, and when called upon, stoically "bear the
brunt of great hostility" (Rumsfeld on Rockefeller) from
those whose policy preferences have been rejected, all the
while subordinating personal preference and shunning
public glory.

Jack Watson offers a strategic rationale for a senior
aide to adopt a neutral policy stance: "If you don't act as
honest brokers . . . you lose your capability to play, you
just ultimately cut yourself out over time. As secretary to

the cabinet . . . my role was to become trusted by the cabinet, so they knew I was not going to double-deal, that I would keep a confidence, that I wasn't going to embarrass them in the press. Over time, you have to build that trust. If you don't . . . they are not going to come to you." If the senior aide succeeds, cabinet heads will come to him for adjudication of their jurisdictional disputes with other departments and to appeal budget cuts by the Office of Management and Budget. Again Watson: "By and large, the only people who are in a position to reconcile, to the extent that it's possible, or referee those problems are the members of the White House staff."

In this vein these senior aides describe their responsibilities. But the observations of their actual performance made by the growing chorus of White House critics outline an entirely different story. While the chiefs talk mostly about coordination, the critics rarely do, except perhaps to point to failures in these traditional duties. Instead, those who report on the White House and those who in an official capacity deal with "the president's men" mostly describe staff as delving independently into matters of presidential management and, even worse, as meddling in politics.

Shortly after leaving the Johnson White House, where he served as a special assistant, George E. Reedy wrote a thinly veiled attack on many of his recent colleagues. But Reedy also argued that the deficiencies in talent he witnessed were endemic to the staff system of the White House office, which he described as "a mass of intrigue, posturing, strutting, cringing, and pious 'commitment' " that elevates sycophants who tell the president what they believe he wants to hear and thereby shield him from opposing views and critical information.[11] One gains the distinct impression that to Reedy's mind the modern White House office bears the responsibility for the disaster that befell Johnson in Vietnam.

Perhaps on firmer ground are those who argue that Nixon's White House organization contributed to the collection of misdeeds known simply as Watergate. Clearly, "the plumbers" who broke into the office of Daniel Ellsberg's psychiatrist were a home-grown product, organized by staff assistant Egil Krogh. It is not clear what Haldeman means when he says that the Watergate cover-up resulted from a failure to follow standard operating procedures. Early on, President Nixon did in fact "staff out" to John Dean, his chief counsel, the task of writing a report that would minimize the appearance of White House culpability. If a president is going to commission a cover-up, calling upon the expertise of his chief counsel would seem the most appropriate of organizational procedures. But in doing so, Nixon gave vital responsibility to someone he barely knew—a serious blunder that contributed heavily to his own undoing. Among the lessons of Watergate that Gerald Ford learned, as Nixon's late-arriving vice-president, one concerned White House staffing: "A Watergate was made possible by a strong chief of staff and ambitious White House aides who were more powerful than members of the Cabinet but who had little or no practical experience in judgment." Ford adds, "I wanted to reverse the trend."[12]

Even during normal times, the routine activities of

---

11. George E. Reedy, *The Twilight of the Presidency* (New York: New American Library, 1970), p. xiv.
12. Gerald R. Ford, *A Time to Heal* (New York: Harper & Row, 1979), p. 147.

modern White House staff tend to receive unfavorable reviews. Drawing upon his experience as President Johnson's head of the Department of Housing and Urban Development, Robert C. Wood argues that "as central staffs become engrossed in subduing outlying bureaucracies . . . operational matters flow to the top . . . and policy-making emerges at the bottom. At the top minor problems squeeze out major ones, and individuals lower down the echelons who have the time for reflection and mischief-making take up issues of fundamental philosophical and political significance."[13] This assessment squares with the numerous stories of difficult personnel situations recounted by the chiefs.

With a perspective gained from twenty-five years as a senior careerist in the Bureau of the Budget, Harold Seidman cautions presidents to learn the limitations of personal staff: "There will be many things a White House staff cannot do or will do poorly." Among these limitations, Seidman and co-author Robert Gilmour offer the following: "[Staff] do not have technical competence and do not have the time to acquire it. . . . The advice they give the presidents and their evaluation of conflicting opinions will inevitably be colored by their own biases. They are disposed to discount objections and to exaggerate potential benefits."[14] Accepting these criticisms as valid, the National Academy of Public Administration recently concluded a major reassessment of the institutional presidency by recommending that future White

---

13. Robert C. Wood, "When Government Works," *The Public Interest* 18 (Winter 1970): 39–51.
14. Harold Seidman and Robert Gilmour, *Politics, Position, and Power*, 4th ed. (New York: Oxford University Press, 1986), p. 83.

House staffs be kept small and removed from substantive policy formulation.[15]

In sum, those who have closely examined the conduct of White House staffers complain that presidential aides are too visible, too numerous, and too likely to usurp managerial responsibilities. Yet those who have occupied the highest rungs in the White House staff profess their beliefs in anonymity, small staffs, and coordination.

Reconciling Creed With Reality

When columnist David Broder jokingly prodded the former chiefs with a "come on guys, let's hear about politics," his gambit reflected the surprise and even mild disbelief that the chiefs' earlier comments had evoked. But Broder managed only to elicit more of the same. The discussants talked about politics, to be sure, but in illustrating their earlier remarks with stories about the political jams modern coordinators get into, they merely strengthened their case. By the end of the session, they had thoroughly subdued the cynics.[16]

---

15. "A Presidency for the 1980s," in Hugh Heclo and Lester M. Salamon (eds.), *The Illusion of Presidential Government* (Boulder, Colo.: Westview Press, 1981), pp. 297–346.
16. For evidence on this score, see David S. Broder, "Ex-Aides Swap Tips on Serving the Boss in the White House," *Washington Post*, January 19, 1986.

Like Broder, we may begin by questioning the adequacy of the venerable creed in describing the behavior of senior aides in the modern White House. The sincerity of the panelists' statements is not at issue; but one may wonder whether the apparent discrepancies between our understanding of their behavior in office and their present-day theorizing originate in the opportunities afforded by hindsight or in the natural human desire to cast one's behavior in the best light. There is also a third possibility, one that accepts the chiefs' renditions as accurate statements of their intentions while in office and seeks a genuine reconciliation of creed with reality. But before examining this last explanation, we need to defrock the other two.

Faulty retrospection

Hindsight offers insight. As Richard Neustadt notes in his foreword, there is one attribute the former chiefs have in common: older and wiser, each is a grizzled veteran of presidential service. They may not have consistently practiced Brownlow's creed during their watch, but over time, while in office or possibly later, each acquired an appreciation of the inherent limits of his office. The merits of Brownlow's prescriptions came to be better understood, perhaps, in retrospect. If so, their endorsements of the creed might offer instruction to future presidential aides.

Another explanation in this vein is that these former chiefs are engaging in collective rationalization: aware that their actions in office exceeded the narrow mandate of neutral coordination, they now seek to legitimize their roles by reinterpreting their motives to fit their procrustean mandate. The creed, grounded in theories of scientific management that fail to recognize politics, cannot provide sufficient legitimacy for the staff's seemingly inevitable forays into the political realm. Indeed, the Progressive reform movement from city hall to the White House can be fairly portrayed as a denial of politics in governance. While those who served on the Brownlow committee fully appreciated the political proclivities and talents of their president, they appropriately limited their effort to improving the president's managerial capabilities. As a result, they offered no rationale for Roosevelt's assistants to act as his political as well as administrative "legs." Since presidents must be acutely political actors if they are to succeed, their aides always remain open to charges of meddling in matters beyond their legitimate domain.

In addition, even in the narrower managerial realm, the creed no longer cloaks staff with sufficient legitimacy to perform the tasks their presidents sometimes give them. As recent presidents have pulled more decisions into the White House, their senior aides wield proportionally broader power.[17] Their political preferences undoubtedly carry great weight with both the president and those seeking to anticipate the president's decisions. And yet the source of the staff's legitimacy remains unchanged: it rests solely on the claim to speak for the president. For an aide to admit to being a manager rather than merely the president's emissary would leave the

---

17. Terry M. Moe describes this trend and gives it a strategic rationale in "The Politicized Presidency," in John E. Chubb and Paul E. Peterson (eds.), *The New Direction in American Politics* (Washington, D.C.: Brookings Institution, 1985), pp. 235–72.

aide vulnerable to direct appeals from agency heads and their clientele. Similarly, for an aide to advocate large specialized staffs would invite charges of staff interference with the prerogatives of officials who have the constitutional and statutory responsibility for policy. Thus the aides' claim of a diminutive role befits their position as actors who have no independent legitimacy. By this rationale, the necessity for self-effacement grows in direct relation to the staff's involvement in management. Perhaps it is this growing imbalance between power and legitimacy in the presidential advisor's role that has elevated what began as a job description to its current status of sacred litany. If so, the retrospection offered here would reveal more about the ambivalent status of modern presidential aides than about their actual performance.

Against these hypotheses, an array of evidence suggests that in office these men acted as though they were following the creed, or thought they were, even when others might claim that they were not. For none of the chiefs is the endorsement of diminution more paradoxical than for Haldeman. He presided over the largest, most centralizing White House so far, and yet here he earnestly espouses professional self-effacement as forcefully as the others. Is he merely voicing a convenient guise or acknowledging a lesson finally learned? Neither, the record suggests. From his earliest days as chief of staff, Haldeman was preaching the gospel of Brownlow to his colleagues. At a staff meeting before Nixon's inauguration, he read aloud Brownlow's words and admonished the staff to share this man's "passion for anonymity." On coordination versus management, he explained to the new staff, "Our job is not to do the work of government, but to get the work out to where it belongs—out to the Departments."[18] Impressed by Haldeman's sincerity, William Safire later wrote that the new chief "honestly thought in the beginning that was the way it could and should be done."[19] One need not search beyond the transcripts presented here for evidence of the sincerity or validity of this creed for modern chiefs. The ease with which these men summon stories from their service vouches for the former, and the verisimilitude of their versions for the latter. Indisputably, in their versions of controversial incidents, they acted as coordinators more than press accounts convey.

Coordination as an organizational responsibility

Another explanation for these chiefs' surprising support for the traditional work ethic would accept their statements as sincere and accurate reflections of their intentions and would look to features of modern White House operations that would allow reconciliation of the venerable creed and the modern reality of presidential governance.

By *coordination* these senior aides are referring to

---

18. Rowland Evans, Jr., and Robert D. Novak conclude: "It showed what kind of aide Haldeman would be, what kind of colleagues he wanted and, most important, who was setting the tone of the Nixon White House." *Nixon in the White House: The Frustration of Power* (New York: Random House, 1971), p. 47.
19. William Safire, *Before the Fall* (New York: Doubleday, 1975), p. 116. Now a *New York Times* columnist, Safire served as a special assistant in the Nixon White House from February 1969 to April 1973.

much more than an individual work ethic. As they see it, ensuring that presidential decisions are not arrived at casually is at least as much an organizational task as it is a personal one for senior staff. Even when stated in personal terms—as when Haldeman sums up his duties as making sure "decisions are arrived at for the right reason," and Rumsfeld recalls the worrisome "oh, by the way" decisions—responsibility for coordinated decision making requires the vigilance of everyone in the White House.

At various junctures in these sessions, participants explicitly state the organizational dimension of protecting the president. Explains Rumsfeld, "You have all these threads, and the White House staff's function is to see that those threads get through the needle's eye in a reasonably coherent way. The staff's job is not to make the decisions, but by the same token, the staff has to avoid letting the president be blind-sided by allowing a single cabinet officer to go out and make a decision."

Addressing the causes of Carter's difficulties with the Democratic Congress, Watson is more specific in identifying the liabilities of weak policy coordination within the White House: "I think the president was involved to too great an extent in too many things. I think we put too many things on the agenda . . . . In terms of organization . . . this seems to be a problem that almost every president . . . suffers from. They go in with an idea that they are going to have a spokes-of-the-wheel staff. There's going to be equal access . . . . That is a fatal mistake . . . . It pulls the president into too much; he's involved in too many things . . . . It also results in a lack of cohesion, a lack of organization."

Judging from the few failures and the numerous narrow misses the chiefs recount, managing the White House—much less the rest of the executive branch—appears to be a full-time job for the staff. Making sure the president is not blind-sided by a forceful cabinet head, staffing out questionable decisions, steering the president clear of potentially embarrassing situations, and coaching him on press relations and public statements would appear to require the elaborate division of labor one finds in the modern White House. The legislative liaison staff must keep the president attuned to sentiment on Capitol Hill. The secretary to the cabinet and various policy advisors must work with the cabinet heads to keep abreast of upcoming policy decisions. Public liaison staff must brief the president on what support he can expect from various organized constituencies and what they in turn expect from him. The press secretary and communications staff prepare the president for encounters with the news media. The list of White House specialists so engaged is a long one.

If the function of the modern White House office is to regulate the exposure of the president to politicians and ideas, the duty of the chief is to see that the process works. Again Rumsfeld: "He has to assure that people do get the opportunity to have their voices heard, but he has to be the one who helps the president maintain a certain discipline and order in the process or else the process loses its integrity."

As chiefs and other senior aides have taken over much of the responsibility for coordinating the business of the White House, they naturally desire from the staff the same dutiful service Brownlow wanted for the president. Haldeman welcomed an assembly of new recruits about to enter presidential service by reading them Brownlow's prescriptions regarding self-restraint and anonymity. This is a work ethic ideally suited to reining in the entrepreneurial urges of junior staff, and it thus provides the senior staff with an essential mechanism for controlling those who occupy the lower rungs of the bureaucracy.

Yet, bureaucratic utility aside, the transcripts make plain that these former chiefs subscribe to the creed as a personal code. That reality appears different may simply mean that good intentions are insufficient. As responsibility for coordinating the president's work shifts from the president to his senior aides, maintaining the low profile of an unobtrusive participant becomes difficult. Reputations sometimes become so tainted with conflict and notoriety, the best an aide can offer the president is an early resignation.

Obviously, not all staffers who are branded as meddlesome politicians in business for themselves are simply misunderstood coordinators. The fine line between managing the affairs of others and coordinating the president's business means that all senior aides will at some point cross over into the realm Brownlow labeled forbidden territory.

Our discussants do not deny this, but they convincingly argue that even the most pristine acts of coordination are certain to get staff members in trouble. In order to supervise the flow of callers and messages to and from the Oval Office, senior aides must make decisions, and their decisions invariably advance some political interests over others. When Haldeman ushered administration economists Arthur Burns, Paul McCracken, or Herbert Stein into the Oval Office so that President Nixon's understanding would not be predicated exclusively on the views of his close friend Secretary of Treasury John Connally, what was Mr. Connally to think? Did he applaud Haldeman for making sure that the president would be able to make the right decision for the right reason, or did he suspect that Haldeman was out to undermine Treasury's position? We do know what Vice-President Nelson Rockefeller thought when Rumsfeld repeatedly reported unfavorably to President Ford on Rockefeller's domestic policy proposals. Beyond the personal hostility that Rumsfeld reports here, Rockefeller railed bitterly against Rumsfeld to one of Washington's most astute president watchers, John Osborne, voicing suspicion that the chief of staff wanted to replace him on the ticket in the next election.[20] By Rumsfeld's account, he was performing thankless duty—serving as Ford's javelin catcher—in order to preserve the friendly relations between president and vice-president; by Rockefeller's account, the coordinator was trying to satisfy his own incontinent political ambition.

One lost virtue begets another. If the exercise of discretion, even in the service of coordination, sometimes suffices to stir up conflict, that conflict in turn is frequently sufficient to raise the public spotlight. Personality conflicts make good copy, of course, but first someone has to decide to escalate the dispute by going public. Almost invariably, it will not be the presidential aide but his or her adversary. Just as Rockefeller took his case against Rumsfeld to Osborne, Secretary Heckler took hers against Donald Regan to Congress and the press.

---

20. John Osborne, *White House Watch: The Ford Years* (Washington, D.C.: New Republic Books, 1977), pp. 214–15.

Two simple facts of political life explain this pattern: Presidential assistants make easy marks, and presidents do not. Frequently, politicians will pick on an aide in order to avoid taking on the president, just as the Democrats on Capitol Hill singled out Communications Director Buchanan to explain their opposition to the president's aid legislation for the Contras. And in an intramural fight described in the third session, a long-term Ford assistant is reported to have tried to change the president's decision to retain some of Nixon's staff by leaking to the press that it was the bad idea of Haig, the holdover.

Without constituencies or statutory authority to sustain them, these transient political actors cannot long stand public controversy. They and everyone else know that however sympathetic the president may be, at some point continued support for a restive aide will be too costly. When Nixon fired Interior Secretary Hickel and Carter initialed the "resignation" of Health and Human Services Secretary Califano, each accepted the political costs of a decision that was unpopular among some constituencies. But when Nixon sacked Haldeman and Carter dismissed Budget Director Bert Lance, colleagues and friends sighed with relief that the president had finally cut his losses. Unlike many other presidential appointees, staff members are expendable.

Thus it is in the strategic interest of senior aides to endorse the circumscribed role of coordinator and aspire for anonymity. Watson's strategic rationale for staff to be perceived as honest brokers, cited earlier, can easily be extended. Staff discretion, exercised most defensibly in the realm of coordination, becomes paramount when disagreements arise. Senior aides will then strive, in

Haldeman's words, to "solve internal problems . . . internally." Such intentions, however, are easily thwarted by antagonists who perceive it to be in their own interest to shift the dispute to the public arena. For the modern chief, then, Brownlow's prescriptions of coordination and anonymity comprise an effective *strategy of action*. But when coordination becomes an organizational task, the stakes—who and what message will get to the president—rise and antagonists can push discreet coordinators into the limelight.

Reconciling the third feature of Brownlow's creed— namely, the virtue of small staffs—with modern practice is another matter. While the presence of other players prevents the chiefs from maintaining the anonymity they prefer, the obstacles to their achieving an intimate "lean and mean" White House result directly from the presidential decision to have the senior staff assume responsibility for running the White House.

The Rationalization of the White House Office

The chiefs preach small staffs but have given us large ones. In this instance the discrepancy between creed and reality cannot be easily relieved by reference to the differing perceptions of those inside and outside the White House. Rather, the discrepancy originates in their very insistence on coordination as the proper domain of the staff. Once responsibility for coordination shifts from the president to the organization, the need for personnel increases sharply. Making sure "all the threads fit through the needle," McPherson reminds us, requires a sizable staff.

Equally important, once the president relinquishes control over running the White House, he in effect releases a strong brake on staff size. Clearly, the staff must remain small if a president is to be his own office manager; otherwise his aides would so monopolize his schedule that he would have little time for matters beyond the White House. Clark Clifford, seeking to reconstruct Roosevelt's system in a transition memo to President-elect Kennedy, stated categorically the organizational principles of presidential self-management: "A vigorous president in the Democratic tradition will probably find it best to act as his own chief of staff, and to have no highly visible majordomo standing between him and his staff. . . . It is important that all the senior professional persons on the staff should have access to the President, and the staff should consist of no more persons that can conveniently have such access on a day-to-day basis."[21] Kennedy subsequently set up just such a system.

Once size is no longer limited by the president's span of control, however, there is a natural tendency for staff to grow. Faced with decisions that must be made despite uncertainty about the preferences of others and little foreknowledge of the consequences, aides begin recruiting help to improve their own competencies. At one moment, Sorensen speaks fondly of the small staff system that gave him and others access to the president, but

---

21. Clark M. Clifford to John F. Kennedy, Memo on Transition, November 9, 1960, John F. Kennedy Library.

when invited to speculate on what he might have done differently, he wishes he had had more help. We may venture that had he been in a White House where coordination fell to the staff, all he would have needed do was ask.

To the degree the discussants endorse coordination as an important organizational goal of the modern White House, they in fact deny the value of a small staff. And once the staff is no longer small, the issue of its management arises, which brings us to a second critical difference between these chiefs' views on the requirements of modern White House management and the plan propagated by Brownlow and practiced by Roosevelt. Removed from the president's responsibility, coordination in the opinion of these panelists (with the exceptions of McPherson and Sorensen) mandates a chief of staff system. Watson's solution to the overload encountered by Carter is unequivocal: "Many of our problems . . . would have been solved had we started from the very beginning with a strong chief of staff."

More than sheer size is involved, for growth has been accompanied by internal differentiation. While such specialization enables the staff to monitor the president's environment more effectively, it also requires the organization to develop internal channels of communication and coordination. To some degree this can be achieved with standard rules prescribing how messages are to be routed. But with the massive turnover of personnel after elections and high continual turnover at other times, routines necessarily hold less sway in the White House than in most other organizations: In an organization of transients, few members have an allegiance to the traditional rules and procedures that is strong enough to outrival the immediate gratifications that may come from breaking the rules. Nor is an organization of transients able to engage in collective enforcement of a time-honored code. In the absence of an authority—collective or individual—who enforces the standard operating procedures, internal coordination breaks down; in the absence of an authority who occasionally overrides procedures, the organization loses its responsiveness. Rumsfeld offers a vivid illustration of the chief's role in a differentiated White House when he describes how speechwriters try to thwart the routing of materials in order to protect their turf: "The chief of staff has to heave his body in the middle and try to figure out a way for the substantive portions of the speech to finally reach the substantive people."

The conception of the White House staff as a hierarchical organization headed by a strong chief and structured by orderly lines of communication embodies the same principles that the Brownlow committee worked from in installing the president atop the executive branch. Although Brownlow and his colleagues warmly endorsed Roosevelt's preference for a small circumambient staff, their call for the partition of the executive's staff functions into formal presidential agencies, such as the Bureau of the Budget, indicates that these advisors were as enamored with the enterprise of rationalizing organizations as were their academic colleagues in the field of scientific management. Indeed, the committee's preliminary draft contained a provision for a cabinet secretariat in the White House, to be headed by an executive secretary who would oversee relations among the secretariat members and with the president. While the inspiration for this office sprang more from a desire to fill the space between the president and the executive departments by adding a suprastructure to the cabinet, in practice this arrangement would not have differed much from the strong-chief system.[22]

But the final report was dictated less by administrative theory than by Franklin Roosevelt. The proposal for a cabinet secretariat turned out to be the only part of the draft report to which he took exception. He predicted that such an executive secretary would become unduly burdened by the attentions of the press, and that the public probably would not stand for it. The president conceded that while in all likelihood one of the aides would emerge *primus inter pares*, he wanted that arrangement kept out of the final report.

When modern chiefs disparage the spokes-of-the-wheel system, they are taking issue more with Roosevelt's views on the presidency than with Brownlow's. Although the debate is never explicit, the recent chiefs frontally dispute the rationale of Roosevelt's system; they disparage his juggling of staff, which created competition among them, and his insistence that all routine tasks (including, remarkably, congressional liaison) be located elsewhere in order to give him maximum flexibility in choosing the issues in which he would become involved. Watson and the other recent chiefs argue that fluid staffing arrangements controlled by the president no longer

22. Writing about this proposal in 1963, Barry Karl concluded, "A modernization of this method could have involved the creation of a highly rationalized bureaucracy located midway between the President and his cabinet." *Executive Reorganization and Reform in the New Deal* (Chicago: University of Chicago Press, 1963), p. 240. See also Peri E. Arnold, *Making the Managerial Presidency* (Princeton, N.J.: Princeton University Press, 1986), pp. 99–107.

promote flexibility but, to the contrary, open the gates of the Oval Office to an uncontrollable inflow of demands. In the deluge, without assistance of the kind a chief provides, the president cannot retain any control over his choice.

While the strong-chief system still remains insufficiently legitimate for these former aides to disembrace "small is beautiful," they do offer a reconciliation of sorts between the venerable creed and the requirements of the modern White House office. In order to preserve Brownlow's system, they jettison Roosevelt's.

Conclusion: The Prospect for Strong Chiefs

The White House is the president's workplace. How any future president will organize the staff will reflect foremost the president's own needs, work habits, style of leadership, and political goals. While biases inherent in the electoral system may favor some types of candidates so as to skew the distribution of the personal attributes of future incumbents, individuality and variety in White House organization will continue to be the norm.[23]

Nonetheless, it is also true that presidents adapt, or

---

23. For consideration of how the presidential selection system favors certain styles of leadership over others, see Samuel Kernell, "Campaigning, Governing, and the Contemporary Presidency," in Chubb and Peterson, *New Direction*, pp. 117–42.

at least react, to changes in the political environment, and several forces at work in contemporary politics may prompt presidents to look more favorably on strong-chief systems. Presidents today work in a setting of enforced activism. Failure to be as involved as the press, other politicians, and the public expect can itself be politically damaging. Within hours after the alert at Three Mile Island, reporters showed up at the White House for a statement. A pilot flew over the *Mayaguez*, and in an instant the entire chain of command turned to the president.

When to join the political fray, of course, has always been an acutely strategic decision. Roosevelt was famous for holding back and awaiting the propitious moment, which sometimes came after others had decided he was too late. But presidents today frequently act as if patience, temporary neutrality, or strategic delay were luxuries denied them. Two examples of the opportunity costs of noninvolvement appear in these proceedings. Sorensen mentions that Kennedy wanted to be fully informed on the operations of U.S. forces in Germany because "he was damned if the question of war with the Soviet Union over Berlin was going to be decided by some sergeant on the border making a decision with respect to a tank or a troop movement." And Haldeman in a brief repartee with John Chancellor notes that if the White House does not select the "message of the day," the networks will. A president who fails to define the political agenda for Congress and the nation leaves a vacuum that will be filled quickly by others in the political marketplace.

Finally, presidential activism is enforced by the new realities of coalition-building in Washington. There are fewer hierarchies in Washington today than in Roosevelt's time, fewer leaders with whom a president can cut a deal and reasonably expect them to be able to enforce it in their agency or committee. Fragmented parties in Congress mean that negotiation with institutional leaders will no longer suffice; even the freshman representative may expect occasional presidential stroking before an important floor vote. Nor can the president rely on atrophying political parties and mediating organizations to help him assemble a governing coalition across the country. The modern president is increasingly on his own when it comes to coalition building, and this enforced self-reliance means increased presidential activity. In the view of the recent chiefs, the demands for activism and the requirements of self-reliance encourage presidents to look favorably upon the kinds of services provided by a rationalized White House run by a strong chief.

These circumstances are forcing presidents to reevaluate lessons from the past—another source of normalcy for organizational styles across administrations. Most presidents have read these "lessons" as instructing them to reject strong-chief systems. Roosevelt, whose shadow has loomed over every one of his successors, succeeded brilliantly by rejecting the concept of the rationalized White House. Eisenhower, by setting up a strong-chief system and failing to show that it could be put to good advantage, reinforced Roosevelt's lesson. How could a president, students of the office ask, require that policy choices be presented to him on a single page and then expect to do more than merely bestow or withhold his blessing on decisions made by others? By strengthening his staff, the president only weakened himself. The famous newspaper headline, "Adams Insists Ike Is Really President" said it all.[24]

And finally, we learn in the remarks of Ford's and Carter's aides about the adverse lessons of Watergate for strong chief of staff systems. That a White House office with clear management responsibilities could be put to the service of an activist president might have been a lesson from Nixon's tenure had any salutary benefits of his staff organization not been discredited by the mischiefs of Watergate.

In direct response to Watergate, Ford and then Carter consciously set out to avoid a strong staff system and instituted a spokes-of-the-wheel approach. Yet three men who worked under the more open system—Rumsfeld, Cheney, and Watson—end up seconding the opinions of Haldeman and Haig: that coordination should be lodged with a strong chief. Their views are so convincingly buttressed by the stories they tell, one would be hard put to argue differently, at least for their presidents. Drafted into the White House, President Ford remained the affable legislator who repeatedly benefited from the protection of Rumsfeld and Cheney and who suffered (as in the case of Secretary of Labor Dunlop) when staff work broke down. Watson's case for a strong chief in the Carter White House is similarly convincing and based on evidence with which few president watchers would disagree. Admittedly, Carter's own disposition may have

24. Fred I. Greenstein, *The Hidden-Hand Presidency* (New York: Basic Books, 1982), p. 139.

been more responsible than his administrative system for pulling decisions into the Oval Office.[25] Nonetheless, Watson's assessment of the drawbacks of the Carter White House rings true. Had some order been imposed on the influx of demands and information, Carter would have stood a better chance of establishing legislative priorities and would have done better in Congress.

Over time, these chiefs' assessments came to be shared by their bosses. Trying to "reverse" the effects of Watergate, Ford began his abbreviated term with an open White House. Within six months, by his own account, he reversed himself: "A President needs one person who at least coordinates people."[26] Carter's conversion was slower but more dramatic. Desperate to restore public confidence, he reorganized his administration, sacking those cabinet secretaries who he said could "not get along with the White House staff," and designating Hamilton Jordan as chief of staff.[27]

Reflecting both the lessons of past presidents and their experience, the professional chief of staff envisioned by Cheney, Rumsfeld, and Watson is one whose function is neither to relieve the president of the burden of making

---

25. As one department official remarked on reading Carter's detailed recommendations on a reform proposal, the president is "the highest-paid assistant secretary of planning that ever put a reform proposal together." Joseph A. Califano, *Governing America: An Insider's Report from the White House and the Cabinet* (New York: Simon & Schuster, 1981), p. 403.
26. Ford made this comment at a conference held on March 25, 1977, and published by the American Enterprise Institute for Public Policy Research as *A Discussion with Gerald R. Ford: The American Presidency.*
27. Jimmy Carter, *Keeping Faith* (New York: Bantam Books, 1982), p. 116.

choices nor to pull more decisions into the White House. The volume and substance of a president's work will ultimately depend more on his goals and energy and the times in which he serves than on the internal organization of the workplace. Instead, they describe a chief whose duties are those of a coordinator—one who prevents the president from being "blind-sided," who makes sure the president "makes the right decisions for the right reasons," and who sees to it that "all the threads get through the needle."

Heightened demands for performance and increasing self-reliance are forcing adaptation. In the process, new lessons that hold strong chiefs in higher regard are replacing old lessons that rejected them as ineffective. Thus far, nothing in President Reagan's experience serves to deny or refute the lessons unfolded during the terms of Ford and Carter.

New prescriptions are being grafted on old. The staff's responsibility for managing the president's work is now an established fact of political life. So, too, are the institutional requirements for a sizable staff and the presence of a central authority to regulate its activities. Only the legitimating creed remains to be developed. Despite appearances, the new adaptations do not entail a repudiation of the venerable creed. The desire for anonymity and the emphasis on coordination, illustrated so fully at this colloquium, will retain their vigor among presidents and senior aides because they continue to offer important strategic benefits. The virtues of small staffs have less value; over time, as staffs stabilize at the current level and the lessons of the past recede, one will no longer hear dutiful expressions of homage to this fragment of the creed.

"The president needs help," proclaimed the Brownlow committee. The chiefs concur. Brownlow offered a
solution befitting the times and the man he served—the
"times" half a century ago, the "man" exceptional. The
reflections and considered judgments of these former
chiefs offer future presidents an alternative, one grounded in the creed of the past but adapted to the demands of
the future.

Samuel Kernell
The Brookings Institution
Washington, D.C.
June 1986

INDEX

Designer: Sandy Drooker
Compositor: Wilsted & Taylor
Text: 10/13 Aster
Display: Aster Bold
Printer: Vail-Ballou Press
Binder: Vail-Ballou Press

353.032 Kernell, Samuel,
KER   1945-

        Chief of staff

$15.95

DATE